C000261921

The
Southern Way

The regular volume for the Southern devotee

Kevin Robertson

Issue 37

www.crecy.co.uk

© 2017 Crécy Publishing Ltd
and the various contributors

ISBN 9781909328617

First published in 2017 by Noodle Books
an imprint of Crécy Publishing Ltd

All editorial submissions to:
The Southern Way (Kevin Robertson)
Conway
Warnford Rd
Corhampton
Hants SO32 3ND
Tel: 01489 877880
editorial@thesouthernway.co.uk

All rights reserved. No part of this book may be
reproduced or transmitted in any form or by any
means electronic or mechanical, including
photocopying, recording or by any information
storage without permission from the Publisher in
writing. All enquiries should be directed to the
Publisher.

A CIP record for this book is available from the
British Library

Publisher's note: Every effort has been made to
identify and correctly attribute photographic
credits. Any error that may have occurred is
entirely unintentional.
In line with the new design the front cover image has
changed from that originally advertised. All other
information is unaffected.

Printed in Slovenia by GPS Group

Noodle Books is an imprint of
Crécy Publishing Limited
1a Ringway Trading Estate
Shadowmoss Road
Manchester M22 5LH

www.crecy.co.uk

Issue No 38 of THE SOUTHERN WAY
ISBN 9781909328624
available in April 2017 at £14.95
To receive your copy the moment it is
released, order in advance from your usual
supplier, or it can be sent post-free (UK)
direct from the publisher:

Crécy Publishing Ltd

1a Ringway Trading Estate, Shadowmoss
Road, Manchester M22 5LH

Tel 0161 499 0024

www.crecy.co.uk

enquiries@crecy.co.uk

Front Cover:
**Flashback to the heyday of steam on the Isle of Wight
under BR. No 16 *Ventnor* with a Cowes line service.
No 16 survived to the very end of steam on the Island
but was destined to be reduced to scrap soon after
withdrawal in 1967. *J. A. Cull***

Rear Cover:
**No, Southern Way has not gone 'all LNER', but look
what it is and especially where it is... ...the interchange
trials of 1948 and the famed LNER No 22 'Mallard'
departing from Waterloo for Exeter on what was a
preparatory 'familiarisation' run before the actual tests
commenced. A fascinating article on the interchange
trials and the performance of the Southern engines
involved will appear in SW38 due in April.**

Title page:
**One of the fabulous images taken by the late Edward
Griffiths, this of M7 No 30049 on a Guildford to Horsham
branch service sometime in 1951 and typical of similar
types of services operating throughout the system at the
time.**

Contents

Introduction

Writing this (well starting it at least) in early September, I am very conscious that while at this precise moment in time it is hot, oppressive and muggy, by the time it is read in January it will likely be the opposite, i.e. cold and wet. Such, of course, is the variability of the seasons but, more to the point, is the need to prepare matters well ahead of publication to allow for sufficient 'lead time'. This applies particularly to the January issue when everything seems to come to a halt soon after the second week in December and thus half the month is effectively lost. Now I am not in any way going to be a killjoy and criticise anyone for having a Christmas break but instead I make the point that what may well be topical and appropriate to discuss at this specific moment in time (September) could have been well and truly usurped four months later.

Indeed I suppose I could bring up the subject of available seating on today's trains especially, as in recent weeks, there was much coverage in the media of 'a certain politician' photographed sitting in the corridor. Fear not, that is as political as I am going to get; ours is a hobby and I am determined to keep it that way.

However, I too had a recent similar experience, three in fact in a matter of two weeks, once on a SWT 'special offer ticket' to Waterloo, when it was standing room only for more than an hour, and then a few days later in both the down and up directions between Salisbury and Exeter. I know others have to endure such situations on a daily basis and overcrowding is certainly not a new phenomenon but it begs the question, and indeed the theme of this editorial, how the passenger (I suppose I should use the word 'customer' these days) is viewed from the perspective of the railway professional, regardless of his role and/or position.

So let us be blunt. We are all 'customers' at some time in our lives and this applies to everything in which we involve ourselves. Customers of the bank we use, the shop we go to, the pub we frequent – the list is endless – and yet if you have ever been the employee 'at the coal face' you will immediately have been aware how difficult some individuals can be and, of course, when seen from the opposite side, how difficult some employees can appear to be. Having experienced both sides, as I am sure most of us have, I have come to the realisation that this confrontation is usually down to a simple breakdown in communication, one party simply unable to explain him- or herself with sufficient aplomb to elicit the service or answer required. It is almost as if the two individuals are running parallel to each other, unable to converge on a cohesive course.

The same applies with railway history. How it is viewed by the enthusiast 'looking in' and how that same history is seen by the professional 'looking out'. I will add there are also any number of professional railwaymen who became professionals because they simply like railways, others later became enthused as a result of their work, while others will have had any of their

Another Guildford–Horsham view, this time of Baynards (between Cranleigh and Rudgwick). Opened on 2 October 1865, it closed amid a howl of protest on 14 June 1965 just a few months short of its centenary. Those campaigning for the railway to remain were convinced the figures had somehow been manipulated, a similar accusation to that being made elsewhere. Whether there was truth in this is really irrelevant now. There have been several calls in recent years for the route to be reinstated to service a commuter need that simply did not exist half a century ago. While it might be thought this would be welcomed, the debate is now over how much further development a reopened railway would encourage. We shall watch this space with interest. Baynards was famed for its horticultural displays, a tradition maintained to the very end of British Railways operation. *Amyas Crump collection*

enthusiasm knocked out of them or regard their role purely as a job – a means of earning a living. I do not condemn any of the latter, for we are all different individuals. I recall too my late friend (and regular SW contributor) Tony Goodyear recounting how early in his own career with the S & T department he had to be very careful not to announce or indeed display his enthusiasm for certain aspects (pardon the pun) of mechanical signalling, as to do so at the time was regarded as career suicide.

At *Southern Way* I am grateful to receive contributions from all. Some are from current or former railwaymen, some enthusiasts, many from each side clearly learned individuals. I have said before that the breadth and depth of knowledge out there never fails to amaze me but one thing also comes out, if a man was a former professional railwayman then often his approach and therefore his view on a specific topic would invariably be different to others.

That is not to say he is also always right. I am certainly not attempting to place anybody on any sort of pedestal but it is interesting to learn sometimes how something that might otherwise just be observed from the platform or public standpoint takes on a totally different perspective when forming part of the daily workload.

Examples here could well be the overcrowding I spoke of at the start. Certain professional railway staff will be 'in the thick of it' probably daily, while others perhaps in a back office function will either be unaware of or conveniently ignore it as not their problem. Turn then to history. As an example, let us say a researcher reports the facts of an incident/machine/location as he or she has been able to ascertain them, yet in reality the true facts may well be very different. Where am I leading, well indirectly to the pages of Rebuilt within this issue and specifically the topic of DEMUs, their usage and the changes that were wrought over the years. Clearly this is a topic that is certainly popular with readers and yet from the correspondence I have received (and still am receiving) it is also the subject of differing views and opinions. Now I am certainly not going to suggest whose opinion is right and whose is wrong; said writers have made contact because they earnestly believe theirs is the true story and they wish their knowledge to be imparted to a wider audience. I am grateful to them, for that is exactly the *raison d'être* of SW. What I cannot say is who is more right than the next man, so make up your own mind but be wary of two lessons from history. The first is the fable of the 'emperor's new clothes' and the second the way an item can start out as fact and yet might be (unintentionally) embellished in the telling as it passes through the hands (and minds) of others.

It is for this reason that on the subject of DEMUs in Rebuilt I have deliberately left out the names of the contributors. This is a first and I do so with absolutely no intention of being controversial or disrespectful. I suspect it probably all started off on the right path, and it may well be that they are reporting what they believe to be 100 per cent accurate, in which case we should perhaps focus on where that actual information came from.

As ever, I await the brickbats.

Kevin Robertson

A distinctly grimy BR 4MT No 80138 arriving at Lymington Town with the 15.58 Brockenhurst to Lymington school train, 20 September 1965.
SWC J. Eyers collection

The Brockenhurst School Trains
(and Some Other Workings ...)

Richard Simmons – ex Southampton Control

<table>
<tr><td colspan="6">MONDAY, 12th APRIL</td></tr>
<tr><td colspan="6">No. 57—Train Alterations and Additions</td></tr>
<tr>
<th>Time</th>
<th>From</th>
<th>To</th>
<th>Remarks</th>
<th>Service No.</th>
</tr>
<tr><td>a.m.
5 40 Q
(Stone Empties)</td><td>Three Bridges</td><td>Wilton South</td><td>Will run. Load: 10 hoppers and brake van</td><td>—</td></tr>
<tr><td>6 55 Q
(Material Empties)</td><td>Salisbury</td><td>Redbridge</td><td>Will run. Load: 40 loaded E.D. wagons and 2 brake vans. (Formed of 2.50 a.m. Sidmouth Jct.).</td><td>—</td></tr>
<tr><td>7 45</td><td>Southampton Term.</td><td>Totton</td><td>Diverted to Eastleigh</td><td>62</td></tr>
<tr><td>7 50</td><td>Bournemouth Ctl.</td><td>Christchurch</td><td>Will not run.</td><td></td></tr>
<tr><td>8 10</td><td>Christchurch</td><td>Brockenhurst</td><td>Will not run.</td><td></td></tr>
<tr><td>8 10</td><td>Lymington Pier</td><td>Brockenhurst</td><td>Will not run.</td><td></td></tr>
<tr><td>8 14 Q</td><td>Bournemouth West</td><td>Waterloo</td><td>Will run</td><td></td></tr>
<tr><td>8 25</td><td>Totton</td><td>Eastleigh</td><td>Will not run.</td><td></td></tr>
<tr><td>8 33
(Freight)</td><td>Eastleigh Yard</td><td>Alton</td><td>Depart Shawford 9.5 a.m. and run 3 minutes earlier to Winchester City.</td><td>—</td></tr>
<tr><td>9 14</td><td>Brockenhurst</td><td>Bournemouth Ctl.</td><td>Will not run.</td><td></td></tr>
<tr><td>p.m.
3 50</td><td>Brockenhurst</td><td>Lymington Town</td><td>Will run to timings shown on page 19 of F.W.T.T.</td><td>—</td></tr>
<tr><td>4 18</td><td>Eastleigh</td><td>Totton</td><td>Will not run.</td><td></td></tr>
<tr><td>4 23</td><td>Lymington Pier</td><td>Lymington Town</td><td>Will not run.</td><td></td></tr>
<tr><td>5 50</td><td>Totton</td><td>Fawley</td><td>Start from Eastleigh M.P.D. at 4 9 p.m.</td><td>59</td></tr>
<tr><td>7 55 (Vans)</td><td>Bournemouth West</td><td>Waterloo</td><td>Revised Winchester Jct.</td><td>67</td></tr>
<tr><td>9 0</td><td>Waterloo</td><td>Southampton Docks</td><td>Pass Eastleigh 10.37 p.m. and run 1 minute later thence.</td><td>—</td></tr>
<tr><td>9 15
(Freight)</td><td>Eastleigh Yard</td><td>Feltham</td><td>Revised</td><td>65</td></tr>
<tr><td>9 30</td><td>So'ton Old Docks (Ocean Terminal)</td><td>Waterloo</td><td>Additional. R.M.S. 'Queen Elizabeth'. (Train No. B.26). 'The Cunarder'.</td><td>66</td></tr>
<tr><td>9 48</td><td>Portsmouth & S'sea</td><td>Eastleigh</td><td>Arrive Eastleigh 10.34 p.m.</td><td>—</td></tr>
<tr><td>9 56
(Freight)</td><td>Bevois Park</td><td>Feltham</td><td>Revised</td><td>69</td></tr>
<tr><td>10 15</td><td>So'ton Old Docks (Ocean Terminal)</td><td>Waterloo</td><td>Additional. R.M.S. 'Queen Elizabeth'. (Train No. B.27).</td><td>68</td></tr>
</table>

Setting the Scene

The stimulus for this piece stemmed from the caption beneath the photograph accompanying John Burgess' interesting article 'The Grid' about the G16 on p77 of SW28, when our editor referred to other school trains and in particular those centred on Brockenhurst. Thus my mind was set thinking, for I remembered these trains from my time working in Southampton Trains Supervision Office (Control) (See Richard's recollections in SW issues 6, 8, 12 and 16.) I came to the conclusion that I should use old-fashioned terms, i.e. put pen to paper, as normally these trains were 'not advertised', meaning they did not appear in the public timetable. Fortunately in my own railway memorabilia I have WTTs covering the SR Southern operating area, more commonly known as the Southampton district as it was renamed in 1962, and its successors covering the period 1949 until the mid-1980s. It follows that information has largely been gleaned from these timetables for that period. To my chagrin, however, I regret now I did not retain copies of steam carriage or engine workings for the era when steam reigned supreme.

An example of the weekly notice suspending certain services. This covered the first week of the 1954 Easter Holiday break with the 08.10 Christchurch–Brockenhurst and 08.10 Lymington–Brockenhurst school trains cancelled, together with the associated 07.50 Bournemouth Central to Christchurch ECS similarly cancelled.

Some information on engine working diagrams is taken from T. S. Bradshaw's Southern Region Operating History Part 3, Wessex (XPress Publishing), although this does relate particularly to 1954. I have included some of these details relevant to this article in order to give, I think, some idea of what class of engine worked what.

Throughout the article the term 'stopper' is used to describe slower all-station trains. The reason for this is that otherwise the more common phrase 'all-station' becomes a misnomer, as such services sometimes did not call at one or maybe more stations along a line of route. Also, although the years under review cover periods when first the 12 hour clock was used then replaced by the 24 hour clock (from the June 1965 timetable) the 24-hour clock has been used throughout. Finally, over the years timings of a number of trains were 'tweaked' by a few minutes here and there mostly for pathway purposes. For example, the 16.07 Brockenhurst–Southampton Terminus was altered to start at 16.05, then 16.08, next 16.06 and finally back to 16.08. For clarity, as the train first comes under notice as the 16.07 this time is used continuously; the minor revisions over the years not being recorded. More major alterations are, nevertheless, noted. Validity of WTTs was from one summer timetable to next year's summer, so reference to – for instance – the 1958 timetable refers to the timetable that commenced that summer and was operative until commencement of the 1959 summer timetable.

Unadvertised

This was the single word description used in WTT column heads of trains not to be found in public timetables, although columns did indicate whether such trains were for workers, scholars or staff purposes. The term 'scholars' was dropped from the 1955 timetable onwards but not quite, as will be seen later. Certainly in the 1960s a few unadvertised trains continued to run on late Sunday evenings and early Monday mornings for members of Her Majesty's forces returning to their bases after leave. Staff trains principally ran in early morning 'small hours' to convey early turn staff to work. Also in these politically correct times in which we live, it must be doubtful if the term 'workers' remains in use, perhaps it should now be 'employees'?

The policy of not advertising a service did create an anomaly in that it is known that at least one service appeared in the public timetable as two separate trains several miles apart – the middle portion of the journey being unadvertised. The train in question was the 06.51 Christchurch–Swanage, which was not advertised between Bournemouth Central (as Bournemouth was then known) and Wareham. It is likely this may have been something to do with workers' hours at the then Royal Navy factory at Holton Heath.

After I started railway employment in 1950 I enquired as to why unadvertised trains were not shown in public timetables. I was told that this made cancellation or revision easier to arrange without having to give too much publicity. Over the years, with the exception of staff trains, a few unadvertised services did creep into public timetables. One such staff train that did see the light of day in the public timetable for summer 1963, was the 05.05 Fareham–Southampton Terminus, but having found brief glory it quickly sank into obscurity by not being included in the winter timetable of the same year or anytime thereafter. The air of secrecy surrounding certain services was not confined to the 1960s either, for in the 1954 winter timetable, apart from staff trains, most were fully advertised in public timetables.

Brockenhurst Services

I shall divide these into three sections: Main Line referring to the Bournemouth main line, Lymington branch (self-explanatory) and Old Road referring to the Ringwood Line, a.k.a. the 'Castleman's Corkscrew'. These services were all to provide transport for pupils attending the then Brockenhurst Grammar School, hence perhaps an explanation of the school's catchment area would be helpful.

Brockenhurst is a small New Forest town located towards the south-west of Hampshire with a main line station that had two lines radiating from it, the Lymington branch and Ringwood line ('Castleman's Corkscrew'), of which only the Lymington line survives. To the north is mainly forest land until the township of Ringwood is reached, to the east is forest and heath land until Ashurst on the western outskirts of Totton, and to the south the larger town of Lymington, mainland terminus of the once railway-owned, but now Wightlink, car ferry to Yarmouth, Isle of Wight. West are the towns (and stations) on the 'Bournemouth Direct', namely Sway, New Milton, Hinton Admiral and the far environs of Christchurch and Bournemouth. From the west, pupils would only originate from the county of Hampshire and not nearby Wiltshire and Dorset and for the same reason as referred to by Nick Stanbury in his comments in 'The Grid' (SW30 p81) relating to those pupils 'out of their county' in Surrey, and where there the school in question was located in Middlesex. The situation under discussion now was a bit different as it involved the borough of Bournemouth.

Originally there were three boroughs within the Hampshire county, Portsmouth, Southampton and Bournemouth, each run completely independently by their own councils and 'nothing to do' with Hampshire! Therefore scholars residing within these towns – only Portsmouth was then a city – were not permitted to attend schools in the county and likewise, scholars from county areas were not allowed to opt for a grammar school in the three county boroughs. Hence the main line school train to Brockenhurst started from Christchurch and not Bournemouth West or Bournemouth Central.

Moving forward briefly, it should be remembered that in the 1970s the then government 'reorganised' local government, resulting in Bournemouth, Christchurch and surrounding areas being hived off from Hampshire and placed in the county of Dorset. The county borough status of Portsmouth and Southampton also disappeared. Here I hope the editor will permit me to refer to the late Michael Wharton, satirist, who wrote regular columns for *The Daily Telegraph* under the pen name of 'Peter Simple' and who described these alterations as "The infamous Heatho/Walkerian local government reforms of 1974". In later years the wheel turned full circle and Portsmouth and Southampton reverted to full unitary authorities once again within Hampshire, but I don't think such alterations would have made too much difference to scholars' journeys as by then grammar school travel had diminished greatly as comprehensive schools became established, replacing many grammar schools, together with relatively local catchment areas. And, of course, the 'school run' in private cars became the vogue. Hopefully this discourse about relationships between schools and local authorities will assist readers in understanding the *raison d'etre* for school train starting points and the station origin of their clientele.

Understandably, school trains ran only during term time and not on Saturdays or Sundays. So far as WTTs are concerned, this would require inclusion of a whole list of dates when trains would not run. The usual practice was therefore to include only the date of the long summer holiday, usually from late July until early September. It was left to district offices to include in weekly P notices cancellation dates for Christmas, Easter, Whitsun and August bank holidays, those being the public holidays in those days, and also half-term. For example, the Southampton district 1954 Easter holiday P notice included a block heading 'Scholars Trains' that listed the trains themselves together with the associated ECS and light engine movements. It showed them cancelled between Wednesday, 14 April 1954 and Wednesday, 21 April 1954.

The Trains Themselves: Main Line

The first WTT in my possession is the 23 May 1949 edition and the first reference to a main line school train is on 8 June 1953, the 08.10 Christchurch–Brockenhurst formed with ECS from Bournemouth Central, although curiously there was no return working at the end of the school day. The likely reason for this is that scholars returning would then use an ordinary service train. Prior to the introduction of the morning train,

travel to school would have been by the 07.30 Bournemouth West–Eastleigh stopper, returning home on the 14.10 Winchester City (as that city's main station was then named) – Bournemouth Central stopper. This service recessed at Southampton Central to follow the 13.30 Waterloo–Weymouth (and Bournemouth West), departing Brockenhurst at 16.19. When the Hampshire DEMUs were introduced in September 1957, the 14.10 Winchester City was revised to achieve inter-regional status by becoming the 12.42 Didcot–Bournemouth Central via the Didcot, Newbury & Southampton line! This revised service was evidently not considered suitable for scholars at the end of the academic day and thus in 1958 came the introduction of an unadvertised 16.15 Brockenhurst–Christchurch with ECS continuing from Christchurch to Bournemouth West or Hamworthy Junction. It should also be said that the 08.10 ex-Christchurch was also unadvertised.

This service pattern continued until the introduction of Bournemouth electrification on 10 July 1967, and we might be forgiven for concluding that this was the likely end of Christchurch–Brockenhurst school trains. Such an assumption proved false, as in the 1973 WTT there appeared an unadvertised 16.23 Brockenhurst–Bournemouth (as Bournemouth Central had by then been renamed following the demise of Bournemouth West) 'scholars service' – the title also having been resurrected. It was formed of a 4VEP running ECS from Eastleigh. Compared with years past, there had been no corresponding up service in the morning. Unfortunately I do not have a 1972 WTT so its exact year of introduction is uncertain, but we know it finally ceased in May 1981 at the conclusion of the 1980–81 timetable. The likely reason for the cessation was the number of grammar schools diminishing as a result of the aforementioned government reorganisation, hence fewer pupils travelled and this made it uneconomic to run such trains. Use of the term 'scholars' ceased again during the period 1974–81, and at the same time no holiday dates were given when the train did not run, just a rather bland column note in the WTT 'Runs during school term only', so it was back to P notices to cancel the service during holiday periods.

As might be expected, views of the actual school train workings are conspicuous by their absence but here is another confirmed service, the afternoon Brockenhurst to Christchurch having just left its destination in June 1957 and now running ECS. The engine is T9 No 30287.
J. W. T. House/Colin Caddy collection

At the beginning of this article I referred to the fact that to the east of Brockenhurst the hinterland consists of forest and heathland resulting, unsurprisingly, in no demand for school trains. I did, however, become aware of one former pupil who travelled from Totton to Brockenhurst to attend the grammar school there. This was the late G. A. (Gerald) Jacobs, who told me he used the 07.46 Eastleigh–Bournemouth Central stopper in the morning but unfortunately never mentioned details of his homeward journey! Trawling through timetables, the only train I found at about school finishing time was another unadvertised service, the 16.07 Brockenhurst–Southampton Terminus, or the 14.20 Weymouth–Andover Junction via Eastleigh and Romsey, which left Brockenhurst at 16.35, both trains calling at Totton. Being at school myself until 1950, my trainspotting time was restricted to Saturday afternoons at Southampton Central, the 16.07 ex-Brockenhurst being 'Saturdays excepted'. However, during half-term and the major holidays I sometimes made a foray to Southampton Central on a midweek afternoon, and recall this train being formed of a 3 LAV set (which also proves that certain terms were not restricted solely to EMUs) and which was announced for Southampton Terminus only but alas, I cannot remember anything about its motive power. It became advertised in the summer 1951 timetable, while a year later the destination was altered to Portsmouth and Southsea. It also survived the initial onslaught of the Hampshire DEMUs and ran until 30 October 1959, when after more DEMUs became available, the Southampton Central–Portsmouth and Southsea section of its journey was dieselised and from 2 November 1959 it was diverted back to its original destination – Southampton Terminus. Survival was, however, limited for it was totally withdrawn from the 1960 summer timetable. For a time in the late 1950s one of my shifts in Southampton TSO finished at 16.40, so enabling me to enjoy this oasis of steam to travel to my home station of Sholing riding in the leading coach and enjoying the 'music' produced by a T9!

Researching for the 16.07 ex-Brockenhurst revealed a conundrum. The 1956 winter WTT supplement, which commenced on 17 September, included an item that this train would make an additional unadvertised stop at Woodfidley Crossing Staff Halt; in the opposite direction the 07.46 Eastleigh–Bournemouth Central would do the same, both stops Saturdays excepted. Neither stop though came to fruition, being cancelled on a SN (Special Notice) before the winter timetable came into effect. The conundrum is that to my knowledge such a halt never existed and I have no knowledge of the construction of one. So what was it for? Certainly a signal box existed at Woodfidley Crossing in semaphore days, being closed on 23 October 1966 upon the introduction of colour light signalling in the area. There is not even road access to the line, being in a remote New Forest location with a large area of grass on the up side favoured for grazing by the local ponies and deer. There was a cottage on the down side, no doubt originally built for the crossing keeper and which from passing trains even today seems to be in both reasonable external condition and also inhabited. Indeed, on

at least one of the end walls a sign, not an original Southern green one, still proclaims the location as Woodfidley level crossing. Is there any reader out there with knowledge or information of plans surrounding this halt?

The Lymington Branch

Contrary to the present situation, in 'school train' days there was more regular tweaking of the Lymington branch timetable and operating dates than on the main line, this arising from the necessity to maintain connections at Lymington Pier with Yarmouth, Isle of Wight, ferry services then operated by the Southern's Shipping & Continental department, later Sealink, and with whom there was close co-operation. Privatisation of course put an end to all that with the advent of Wightlink. Currently times of ferry sailings are not even included in South West Trains timetables, an example of 'nothing to do with us, that's the firm next door'.

M7 No 30029 at Brockenhurst with a Lymington branch train, 30 April 1956. Note the spare pull-push set in the background. Two regular pull-push workings operated from this station, those to and from Lymington having the single headcode disc in the centre of the buffer beam, while local trains routed via the 'old road' (the 'Castleman's Corkscrew') displayed a single disc on the right-hand side of the buffer beam. *T. Molyneaux/KR collection*

Back in the 1950s pull & push (P&P)-fitted M7 0-4-4Ts monopolised the majority of branch trains. WTTs indicated such trains with a black star heading the column but – no doubt resulting from a BR dictum – by 1955 the term 'pull and push' minus the black star ceased to be used, and was superseded by a term even more historic, 'rail motor'. By 1965 rail motor also ceased to be used, this time arising from the gradual withdrawal of the faithful M7s and their replacement by non P&P-fitted tank engines. As photographs of the period testify, as electrification drew near, it was not unusual for tender engines to be used, which suggested a situation of using anything capable of turning a wheel. On shorter P&P runs with frequent running round of trains, one can imagine much cursing from footplate crews.

The first appearance of a dedicated, unadvertised school train from Lymington Town to Brockenhurst at 08.30 was in the 1950 WTT and not noted as a P&P working. Before that, presumably scholars had to travel on the 08.05 Lymington Town–Brockenhurst P&P train. At the same time, a 16.01 non P&P Brockenhurst–Lymington Town service was introduced running in school terms only. The starting station of the morning train seems to have been a variable location, sometimes commencing from Lymington Pier at 08.00 and standing at Lymington Town for some eighteen minutes or sometimes running as ECS between Lymington Pier and Lymington Town. A similar situation affected the afternoon service. I have not attempted to list such alterations as they did not affect the principal reason for running these trains, e.g. scholars. This service pattern continued until electrification, although steam traction on the branch including the school trains was replaced by a Hampshire DEMU from 3 April 1967, including school trains. At the time, the Lymington branch held the melancholy distinction of being the last steam branch, and a suitable headboard was carried or chalked upon at least one branch locomotive. Upon electrification, the Lymington branch was worked by a 2HAP EMU with a dedicated school train only in the morning, departing Lymington Town at 08.27. Return home at the end of the school day was by the 16.08 Brockenhurst–Lymington Town ordinary service. As already mentioned I do not have a 1972 WTT but the 08.27 ex-Lymington Town does not appear in the 1973 WTT. So had it already been discontinued in the 1972 timetable? The aforementioned 16.08 Brockenhurst–Lymington Town ended at the conclusion of the 1973–74 timetable.

With regard to rolling stock and motive power provision, until about the mid- to end-1950s some examples still remained of venerable corridor stock of L&SWR origin. References in stock notices to 99, 338 or 410 types indicate inclusion of such stock in those sets. When the Lymington school trains were cancelled during school holidays, P notices referred to the stock either as the six-set or six-set 338, but by 1956 the set referred to was 437. Had the L&SWR stock succumbed and was 437 Maunsell stock? A report in *The Railway Observer* No 355, p285, for September 1958 records that six-set No 99 had been brought out of store for working Hampshire local services, thus suggesting it had ceased to be employed on school trains. The local services referred to were most likely steam relief workings to the DEMUs. The school train stock was berthed overnight at Lymington Pier, although study of LE and ECS movements shown in WTTs over the years indicated that on summer Friday evenings this stock was moved to Brockenhurst and back to Lymington Pier on Monday mornings, this in order to provide berthing space for the through Waterloo-Lymington summer Saturday trains.

Motive power provision was somewhat more complicated as an engine other than the branch M7 was required to position school train stock as this normally did not form any other branch train. Until the end of the 1955–56 timetable, the 07.04 Brockenhurst–Lymington Pier branch service was classified in the WTT as being a mixed train and was worked by two locomotives throughout to Lymington Pier, a T9 (Bournemouth duty 403) and the branch M7. How much freight traffic was conveyed on this service is unknown as no indication is shown in either passenger or freight WTTs. Of course, only vacuum-fitted wagons could be conveyed and it was very likely restricted to Lymington Town traffic off the two overnight freights from the London area, the 22.40 Nine Elms–Weymouth and 22.45 Feltham–Bournemouth Central yard. (This is also where photography becomes difficult, as it would need somebody 'in the know' to recognise that this double-headed and 'mixed' train was worth recording.) We may conclude that the freight aspect of this mixed train consisted solely of traffic deemed too important to wait for the normal branch freight service, which did not leave Brockenhurst until 12.36. Which of the two locomotives detached the freight wagons is unknown as the 07.04 ex-Brockenhurst was only allowed three minutes' station time (I loathe the term 'dwell' time) at Lymington Town. Having reached Lymington Pier the M7 and P&P set returned to Brockenhurst without the T9 at 07.39.

Meanwhile, the aforementioned 16.01 Brockenhurst–Lymington Pier which, to complicate matters, terminated as a passenger train at Lymington Town on those dates when there was no connecting Isle of Wight ferry, continued empty to Lymington Pier as a curious formation. Headed by a Bournemouth 'Q' (416 duty) then the 'school' 6-set plus P&P set, with P&P 'M7' on rear. Upon arrival at Lymington Pier, the 'M7' & P&P set quickly detached and very promptly returned as the 16.18 back to Brockenhurst. Meanwhile, at Lymington Pier the 'Q' berthed the 6-set and scuttled back to Lymington Town to work the 16.40 freight to Brockenhurst. This rather complicated procedure probably altered at the end of the 1954–55 timetable as by the 1955–56 timetable the freight had been retimed to start at 14.50, using the same engine that originally ran light from Lymington Town to Brockenhurst to head the 16.01 passenger. Thus, when arriving at Lymington Pier on the 16.01 from Brockenhurst, it continued back to Brockenhurst. A complicated scenario, certainly, but an efficient use of resources! So ends the tale of Lymington branch services.

An 'old road' pull-push departing from Holmsley on the final leg of the journey to Brockenhurst. No 30108 was recorded on 9 August 1963 at a time when the engine had just nine months of life left and the railway through Holmsley a similar lifespan. *T. Molyneaux/KR collection*

The 'Old Road', aka the Castleman's Corkscrew

Via the old road, scholars were conveyed to Brockenhurst from Ashley Heath Halt, Ringwood and Holmsley, those being the stations on the line in the county of Hampshire, and travelled on the 06.35 Weymouth–Brockenhurst via Ringwood, returning home on the 16.07 Brockenhurst–Bournemouth West via Ringwood.

The 06.35 from Weymouth was a curious train, having developed as a through service over the years and the combining of several non-related trains. It is likely its origins can be traced back before the beginning of World War II, when the Southern Railway 1939 summer timetable included a 07.05 Dorchester (as Dorchester South was then known)–Broadstone service, returning at 08.07. The next public timetable I have is for the winter 1947–48, the last such publication produced by the Southern Railway. By then, the 07.05 from Dorchester had been brought forward to 07.00 and was now extended to Wimborne, returning from there at 08.00. The summer of 1950 saw the 07.00 from Dorchester continuing to run but according to the public timetable still terminating at Wimborne. However, this was not the true position, as it now continued through to Brockenhurst under the 'unadvertised' banner and in the capacity of a school train. (What is now certain is, if a regular passenger wished to travel on, they might be permitted to remain. This would well apply to the other services mentioned.)

There was also a school train before 1950, the May 1949 WTT including an unadvertised 07.59 Wimborne–Brockenhurst P&P service arriving at destination at 08.37, but it was not designated as being specifically for scholars. Prior to 1950 there was an 07.14 unadvertised Brockenhurst–Wimborne workers' P&P, which from June 1950 continued on to Bournemouth West but still remained unadvertised between Brockenhurst and Wimborne. From June 1953, however, it lost its anonymity by being advertised throughout. It is logical to conclude that when the 07.14 ex-Brockenhurst terminated at Wimborne at 07.53 it formed the 07.59 return to Brockenhurst. From commencement of the 1954–55 winter timetable on 20 September, the Dorchester train started back from Weymouth at 06.40 throughout to Brockenhurst and so remained in this guise until the line closed. In 1954 motive power for this train was an Eastleigh 'Q' 0-6-0, having reached Dorchester in the early hours on the previous day's 21.20 (1949 time) Eastleigh–Dorchester freight. While all these shenanigans were going on, there was no replacement service for the 08.02 Wimborne–Dorchester.

The scholars' afternoon homeward journey was on the 16.05 Brockenhurst–Bournemouth West P&P train that, apart from minor timing amendments over the years, was not subject to such complicated revisions experienced by morning trains. However, the description of this being a P&P

train ceased by 1959, probably due to heavy loading that taxed the capacity of a P&P set. Such a deduction seems to be borne out by the fact that on p208 of Brian Jackson's *Castleman's Corkscrew, Part 1* is a photograph of this train on 15 July 1960 and by now leaving Brockenhurst at 16.15, depicting 'Q' 0-6-0 30539 passing Broadstone signal box with a train formed of a P&P set and three-set behind.

So what happened when the line closed? Again referring to Brian Jackson, he reports this time on p155 that four 39-seater buses were required to transport scholars to and from Brockenhurst. In my timetable collection I have a 'Hants & Dorset Motor Services' timetable dated May 1972 'until further notice'. I have no recollection now why I retained it but it is fortunate that I did, because it includes service 130, which operated on schooldays only between Ashley Heath and Brockenhurst Grammar School. No dates of school holidays are included, thus giving the impression that the general public was not encouraged to use it. The route started from Ashley Heath station (still referred to as such) at 08.05, serving Ringwood station (again, referred to as such), Holmsley Old Station (why this station is referred to by that term is unknown) and arriving at Brockenhurst College (note, not Grammar School) and Brockenhurst Waiting Room, which was near to the station, at 08.52. In the afternoon buses started from Brockenhurst College at 16.15, going on to the Waiting Room and back to Ashley Heath station to arrive at 17.05, The service terminated at St Leonards four minutes later, but it was noted that the morning journey was not starting from or serving St Leonards. So Brockenhurst Grammar School became Brockenhurst College and being in Brockenhurst one day during the 2015 summer, I walked to the college gate bus stop to see if any bus route was advertised as serving the Ringwood area. There wasn't, the only route timetable on display was the hourly Southampton–Lymington one. There may, of course, have been a bus plying to and from Ringwood, but it could have been on a private hire basis and so, to use the railway term, 'not advertised'.

While that concludes the chronicles of the Brockenhurst trains, some other interesting points emerge from research into them. For instance, what purpose was served by running a solitary train from Dorchester to Broadstone or Wimborne and back is unknown. Was it because so few trains, either passenger or freight, traversed the Broadstone–Hamworthy Junction single line section and this was done to retain train crew knowledge of this section of line? The time of day these services ran also suggests it was operated by Dorchester crews. I also accept that by suggesting that a train running from before the outbreak of World War II hostilities formed the origin of a Weymouth–Brockenhurst service requires a very lengthy stretch of the imagination, but even so, demonstrates how some services evolved, sometimes over many years.

Before proceeding any further, let us pause and look a bit more deeply at the Broadstone–Hamworthy Junction section of line. Originally part of the 'Corkscrew', its importance shrank after the 'filling in' of the railways in the Bournemouth/Poole area (notably the 'Bournemouth direct'), so taking most direct traffic away from the Ringwood line. Thus it languished until the Southern Railway saw fit to single it on 11 December 1932. In the final ten years or so of its existence it really carried no more than one passenger train each way together with a handful of freights, passenger services being the 03.52 Salisbury–Dorchester passenger and newspaper train, the newspapers being in a single bogie van detached from the renowned 01.25 Waterloo– West of England passenger and newspaper train. Following revision from the 1954 winter timetable it had a ten minutes' earlier start from Waterloo, which in turn had an impact on the 03.52 Salisbury–Dorchester, which was revised to start at 03.25. This train was extended to Weymouth from the 1949 summer timetable, but that immediately begs the question, how did newspapers reach Weymouth before then? Possibly it was via the Great Western route. Post-1949, the empty newspaper van from Weymouth returned via Waterloo to Clapham Yard next to the engine on the 11.30 Weymouth–Waterloo.

The solitary up train over the single line was the aforementioned Dorchester–Broadstone/Wimborne service but there was one other up train to be found in the 1939 summer timetable, which continued until the end of the 1950 summer service. This was the 19.30 Dorchester–Eastleigh via Ringwood designated as passenger and milk, which raises the query, the milk presumably in churns rather than tanks? It was also booked to wait at Ringwood from 20.26 to 20.40, so suggesting something happened there. (This cannot have been a pathway at Ringwood as the Corkscrew was double track throughout. Might it have been held here pending a path to join the main line a few miles further east at Lymington Junction?) At Eastleigh the train connected into the 19.48 Weymouth–Basingstoke, which ran through to Reading General (as Reading was known in those days) from the summer of 1951 by combining with an already existing Basingstoke–Reading General local service. The whole character of the 19.30 ex-Dorchester by running via Ringwood suggests its principal purpose was to convey parcels, mails and other passenger rated traffic to London and destinations via Reading. Upon withdrawal it was replaced by extending the existing 20.50 Bournemouth West–Wimborne WSX/West Moors WSO to Brockenhurst, connecting there into the 19.48 Weymouth–Basingstoke. Meanwhile, the 20.50 ex-Bournemouth West was extended again in the summer of 1955 from Brockenhurst to Eastleigh.

The number of trains traversing the Broadstone–Hamworthy Junction single line did increase a little during summer seasons. To cater for seaside trippers, many of whom would have doubtless purchased weekly holiday Runabout tickets (remember those?), from 1953 during high summer – basically the annual schools' six-week summer holiday period – Saturdays excepted an 09.05 Salisbury–Weymouth (via Fordingbridge) service was introduced, returning from Weymouth at 18.20. This working with minor timing variations continued until 1963, being the last summer prior to line closure. A cynic could be forgiven for saying this move was in preparation for total closure in the following year.

From the summer of 1956 until 1961 inclusive, again Saturdays excepted, this was supplemented by an 08.50 Salisbury–Swanage through train returning at 18.05. Sundays got a look in for one year, 1956, with an 09.30 Salisbury–Weymouth, returning at 18.20. From 1957 until 1962 this Sunday train ran from Eastleigh to Swanage via Ringwood. Other services using the single line on summer Saturdays, taking 1962 as an example, were the 07.57 Waterloo–Weymouth Quay Channel Islands boat train, the 09.15 and 10.54 Waterloo–Swanage, the 11.34 Swanage–Waterloo and finally the 14.45 Weymouth Quay–Waterloo boat train. In contrast, the 1967 Ian Allan printed facsimile of the L&SWR 1914 summer timetable showed eight down and seven up trains on weekdays and three down and one up train on Sundays over the single line. This number includes the forerunner to the latter day of the down and up Waterloo–Dorchester mail trains, which ran via Ringwood with a Bournemouth Central portion detached and attached at Brockenhurst to down and up trains respectively. Both trains in the forerunner and latter day category ran to remarkably similar stopping and timing patterns, including reversing at Southampton Town, as Southampton Terminus was known in those days, until that station closed in 1966.

With regard to freight traffic, for a relatively short stretch of single line – some three miles – a total of two private sidings must be unusual. Both were served in the up direction from the Hamworthy Junction end. The first was Lytchett Siding, followed by Dorset Clay Products' siding. Taking the June 1958 freight WTT as an example, each were served by the then 14.55 Hamworthy Junction, later 10.00, Dorchester South–Millbrook. The stop at Lytchett Siding soon disappeared, believed to have been on 3 November 1958, and Dorset Clay Products' siding did not appear in the June 1959 WTT. Other up freights were the 15.40SX Dorchester South/18.15SO Hamworthy Junction–Bevois Park. In the down direction there was one solitary train, 06.15 Brockenhurst–Dorchester South or Weymouth. In those days, with much freight rationalisation already in progress, regular revisions were being made to freight trains with regard to their starting and termination points and timings.

Forming part of the Pool–Broadstone–Hamworthy Junction triangle, the single line was also used when required to turn locomotives, so avoiding having to go to Bournemouth MPD and back through the Poole–Bournemouth section, which could become congested at times. Also, to cater for the Channel Islands tomato season, many empty vanfits were ordered to Weymouth. But in early and late seasons a surplus of these wagons came about at Weymouth and they were quite often worked to Southampton Old Docks (as the Eastern Docks were then known), requiring special trains either by pre-planned or short notice control arrangements. Many such trains were routed via the single line and Ringwood, not only to avoid the busy Poole–Bournemouth area, but also if they were to be a full load to obviate the requirement of a banking engine on Parkstone bank.

At this juncture, it is likely that some readers will be of the opinion that such ramifications, such as looking at traffic levels on this particular single line, have no remit in an article about school trains. To this point I contend that when giving such consideration to routes such as the Old Road, now having been closed for such a lengthy period of time, that memories become hazy and correspondingly sketchy. It is therefore interesting to delve into their circumstances to remind ourselves of their fortunes and otherwise before closure. In the case of this single line, and with so little traffic using it towards the end, it is perhaps unusual it survived until the whole route, together with the Fordingbridge line, was closed in one go.

And Some Others …

Totton–Eastleigh. This train conveyed pupils from the Totton area attending Eastleigh County High School, commencing running – not advertised – with the 1955 winter timetable on 19 September. It departed Totton at 08.25, returning from Eastleigh at 16.18; both non-P&P trains. Initially it called at Southampton Central, although there can only have been a few passengers on and off taking into account the 'Berlin Wall'-type imaginary barriers that existed at county and borough council boundaries, as explained earlier. Hence, Totton schoolchildren could not attend schools in adjacent Southampton. These trains entered the full public domain when they were advertised in the 1957 summer timetable. From the winter timetable of that year a stop was introduced to the morning train at St Denys. This was doubtless to cater for scholars from such stations as Netley who attended the same school at Eastleigh. I know right from the time I commenced railway employment in 1950 at Netley booking office, there were thirty or so schoolchildren who travelled from Netley to this school, and before each term commenced I had to prepare their season tickets from information received from Hampshire County Council. The 1957 winter timetable saw introduction of the Hampshire diesels with consequent large scale revision to local services in the area. Hence, children from Netley would have travelled on the 07.42 Portsmouth and Southsea–Southampton Central DEMU, changing at St Denys into the train from Totton; no such St Denys stop was made by the afternoon train. From the 1958 winter timetable the morning train called at Swaythling as well. The afternoon train was discontinued from the start of the 1960 summer timetable but the morning train continued, starting from Southampton Central at 08.30 as a steam train and becoming a DEMU at the start of the 1962 timetable. That was not the end of the story, however, as will be seen later.

However, before that, a look at locomotive and rolling stock provision starting with motive power. For the morning train a light engine departed Southampton Terminus at 07.46, had a five-minute water stop at Southampton Central and then went on to Totton. After working the afternoon train, the engine remained at Totton, leaving light engine at 17.50 to Fawley after the 17.12 Fawley–Andover Junction via Eastleigh cleared the Fawley branch single line. During school holidays when the 16.18 ex-Eastleigh did not run, this engine ran light from

A literal pull-push working with a brace of M7s, Nos 30032 and 30031, departing Eastleigh with at least one LSWR three-set. The headcode indicates a Totton–Fawley bound service. *J. Bailey*

Eastleigh to Fawley to work the 18.43 Fawley–Alton (summer)/Winchester City (winter) passenger train. The engine was usually a BR Standard Cl3 2-6-2T but no doubt a 'Mickey Mouse' Ivatt Cl2 2-6-2T deputised when necessary.

Rolling stock used was a little more difficult to determine. I have already explained it was not a P&P train, but in the back of my mind for at least part of its existence I thought it was formed of a Turnchapel 'gate' set, thus making it an unusual formation. I have only seen one rather indistinct photograph (from where I cannot now recall) of the 16.18 from Eastleigh passing St Denys on 4 October 1957 hauled by 2-6-2T No 82014, but there seems to be a third coach on the rear of the train. The outline of the other two coaches does suggest it was unusual, but I was unable to find any evidence of Turnchapel sets being employed on this train. I did find that both had worked on the Callington branch in the 1950s, with No 361 withdrawn in 1956 while No 373 survived re-varnishing in Lancing Works and lasted until 1960.

The eventual answer as to what was used on this service was to be found on p196 of the *Railway Observer* for July 1957, which painted a rather picturesque scene of Sheppey articulated set No 513 leading a leisurely existence working Totton–Eastleigh school trains. I came across two withdrawal dates for this set, one quotes November 1957 and the other June 1958. Companion set No 514 was used on the Salisbury–Idmiston Halt workers' service but the September 1958 *Railway Observer* noted that it was working in the Southampton area, thus indicating that when No 513 was withdrawn, No 514 was transferred from the Idmiston Halt trains to the Totton school train, being withdrawn in October 1959. I'm sure many readers will recall that, following withdrawal of the Queenborough–Leysdown service in 1950, this venerable stock was employed on the Clapham Junction–Kensington Olympia 'Kenny Belle' services.

Another unique feature about the Totton–Eastleigh trains was that during the period they were advertised, timetables

denoted them as conveying third class (as it then was) only accommodation; more evidence that unusual stock was used. On the SR outside the London suburban area and on the Sheppey Light Railway and Turnchapel branch, trains conveying third class accommodation only were principally restricted to newspaper trains running in the 'wee small hours' and which included one or two coaches to accommodate passengers. So I think it is safe to assume that during the period the Totton–Eastleigh trains were not advertised, first class accommodation was unavailable. Also, no pathways were included in WTTs for stock to be worked from Totton to Eastleigh on Friday evenings for maintenance or return to Totton on Monday mornings. Presumably then, any required maintenance was undertaken when the stock slumbered at Eastleigh while scholars were at school.

You will recall earlier in this article I hinted that it was not the end of the story when these trains were discontinued. After a gap of some twenty years in 1979 came what may be described as a mini metamorphosis in that a morning – but not an afternoon – service was reinstated. This came about by using the locomotive, an EDL; stock off the 02.45 Waterloo–Bournemouth passenger; and newspapers that had continued as ECS from Bournemouth and Poole before going to Eastleigh. This ECS train terminated at Brockenhurst to form an 07.56 Brockenhurst–Eastleigh calling at all stations except Beaulieu Road and the then-named Southampton Airport – now Southampton Airport Parkway. It was withdrawn in this form at the conclusion of the 1986–87 timetable, being replaced by an 07.25 Bournemouth–Eastleigh stopper most likely to have been formed with the aforementioned ECS from Poole. Between Brockenhurst and Eastleigh it was closely followed by another stopper, the 07.56 Lymington Pier–Eastleigh. Nevertheless, some perceived requirement must have existed for a train at about the same time as the Totton–Eastleigh service but was it for schoolchildren? Surely the grammar school abolition programme was well under way by the early 1980s?

So to the Finale – for Some Others

Dorchester. Discovery of a service from Weymouth to Dorchester in the morning returning after school hours was purely coincidental. I was thumbing nonchalantly through a WTT when my eyes alighted on the word 'scholars' at the head of a timing column. For this was way after the noun had gone out of fashion in WTTs, but nevertheless was above an afternoon service from Dorchester West to Weymouth. Curiously, there was such a requirement for a school train in deepest sylvan south Dorset, bearing in mind Weymouth is a bustling seaside resort in its own right and would surely have its full quota of schools with no need to move pupils to adjoining towns. Still, Dorchester being the county town of Dorset, it clearly had a school(s) that drew clientele from surrounding areas. The concern to me was that, while working in Southampton Trains Supervision Office (Control), I was on No 4 area, which included Dorchester and Weymouth until displaced when the line from Castle Cary to just short of Dorchester West was transferred back to the Western Region (WR). And this train was running at the time of transfer, although now I have no recollection of it – the ageing memory again!

Following transfer of this line from the WR to SR, the existing steam-hauled service continued, but could not have been considered as frequent. Together with the Maiden Newton–Bridport branch, services on the line, although not to a Sir Herbert Walker 'clock face' principle, improved greatly but still not to regular intervals following introduction on 15 June 1959 of a DMMU scheme based on Bristol. Inevitably, rationalisation has taken its toll with line singling over lengthy stretches together with closure of a number of intermediate stations and the Bridport branch closed completely, plus a reduced service to currently (April 2016) a rather paltry eight trains per day provided by GWR.

The poser: Woodfidley Crossing box east of Brockenhurst. No evidence has been found to support the idea of a halt here although certain local services did call briefly to deliver water in cans – as witness the containers seen. Often such deliveries were made by a regular pick-up goods service so this would seem an unlikely means of transport for schoolchildren. As mentioned in the text, there were some railway cottages nearby although this did not appear to warrant a staff halt – although a few miles away at Alderbury Junction between Salisbury and Dean there was such a provision. *John Bailey*

Before nationalisation not unnaturally both the SR and Great Western Railway named their individual stations in the town 'Dorchester', the suffixes 'West' and 'South' being added to respective stations in 1949, the SR including it from their winter timetable of that year. Going back to Southern Railway days, the respective table in their timetable included a footnote against Dorchester that it was more than ¼mile to the GW station. This footnote, along with many other similar snippets of information, disappeared from public timetables in the summer 1955 edition when the format changed to what became the familiar larger page size. Checking my now rather dilapidated copy of *Bradshaw's* for January 1948, it is interesting to find that the Weymouth line GWR table – which interestingly refers to Weymouth as Weymouth (Town) – gives no such similar information as to the distance between their station and the SR one at Dorchester. Perhaps the GWR still preferred to ignore the intrusion of the (then) Southampton & Dorchester Railway into Dorchester way back in 1847!

SR WTTs never included WR services into and out of Weymouth, and likewise I don't know if WR WTTs included SR trains in theirs. That is until the Castle Cary–Weymouth line was transferred wholly to the SR by inter-regional transfer in 1958. So it is not known if any school trains operated before that date between Weymouth and Dorchester West. What is known is that the SR ran none to and from Dorchester South. But adding a caveat to that, a school train between Dorchester West and Weymouth came about at a rather late stage, not seeing the light of day until the 1960 summer timetable. This followed withdrawal at the end of the 1959–60 winter timetable of the 12.30 Paddington–Weymouth, which departed Dorchester West at 16.12 (public time) non-stop to Weymouth and so was convenient for the end of school lessons. By the way, in the winter of 1958 the SR produced a WTT supplement to include all trains between Castle Cary and Weymouth, the supplement being fully incorporated as part of the main Southampton district WTT the following summer. So after that digression let us return to school trains.

As this particular train did not start life until the 1960 summer timetable and throughout its existence was subject to numerous revisions, I think it will be clearer to deal with it on a year by year basis rather than in paragraph form, so here goes!

1960 – summer. As has already been explained, following the discontinuation of the 12.30 Paddington–Weymouth, to cater for school children an unadvertised 16.15 Dorchester West–Weymouth was introduced calling at all stations and was also a steam train in what was then a sea of DMMUs. I wonder how many youngsters approved? There was no comparable up train from Weymouth in the morning, scholars travelling by existing ordinary services, namely the 08.15 Weymouth–Bristol, which called additionally at Radipole Halt and Upwey and Broadwey. There existed a 10.40 Weymouth–Dorchester West and upon arrival at its destination the engine returned LE to Weymouth, leaving the stock behind to form the afternoon school train.

1960 – winter. The 10.40 Weymouth–Dorchester West was discontinued. Provision of resources for the afternoon train has been well-nigh impossible to determine so some supposition has been necessary. To start with, there was no ECS working from Weymouth to Dorchester West for the school train, but an engine seems to have become available after morning freight shunting at Dorchester South and West and wagon transfer between the two. It has been virtually impossible to establish where the stock came from, the only possibility seemed that it was attached to the 14.07 Weymouth–Swindon parcels for detachment at Dorchester West. However, this theory was thrown out of the window when from 5 March 1962 this train was revised to start at 14.00 and convey passengers between Weymouth and Yeovil Pen Mill, calling additionally at various stations and halts en route and including a stop on Thursdays at Bincombe Tunnel signal box to set down stores. As Thursday was pay day on BR no doubt the 'stores' included signalman's pay packets to this otherwise rather remote location. Nevertheless, it does prove the train included passenger carrying vehicles but were there carriages to form the school train?

1961 – summer. No change.

1961 – winter. The 08.40 Weymouth–Maiden Newton steam service was retimed to start at 08.23, though why so closely behind the 08.15 Weymouth–Bristol DMMU is a mystery but it did give scholars a choice of train.

1962 – summer and 1962–63 – winter. No change.

1963 – summer. A major revision took place when this timetable was introduced on 17 June with withdrawal of the 08.23 Weymouth–Maiden Newton. Replacement was in the form of an additional unadvertised steam train for scholars, 08.23 Weymouth–Dorchester South. To balance, the 16.15 Dorchester West–Weymouth was revised to start from Dorchester South at 16.15. Presumably the change of station at Dorchester made no difference to scholars, with the school easily accessible from both. Hopefully at the end of the first day of station change scholars made their way to the correct station … . There was one further twist: in the WTT the morning train to Dorchester South was shown to run until 19 July only with no autumn term recommencement date, but the afternoon train was shown to recommence running on 17 September when the autumn term began.

1963–64 – winter. As 1963 summer, but with 08.23 Weymouth Dorchester South running and not advertised.

1964–65 – summer and winter. A settling down period with both the 08.23 Weymouth–Dorchester South again shown as running and continuing unadvertised

A reminder of what the school (and other trains) were like. M7 No 30111 propels its train away from Lymington Town, the fireman perhaps either just having 'put a bit round' or even deliberately attempting to liven the fire up a bit. *Dennis Calender*

1964–65 – summer and winter. A settling down period with the 08.23 Weymouth–Dorchester South and 16.15 return continuing as before, but with the 'scholars' designation reappearing in the WTT. Here it should be explained that with closure of the Southampton district office at the end of September 1963, responsibility for WTT production, etc, had passed to the South Western Division Line Manager's organisation at Wimbledon. Was resumption of the 'scholars' term (pardon the pun) a policy change? If it was it was short-lived, as will be observed in 1965.

1965 – summer. A further change revising the 08.23 Weymouth–Dorchester South to start at 08.15, becoming advertised and diverted back to Dorchester West! The 16.15 Dorchester South–Weymouth was withdrawn and covered by the 14.55 Bournemouth Central–Weymouth starting at 14.57 and reposing at Dorchester South from 16.03 to 16.15, thus providing scholars with a homeward service. Although not during school hours, a 17.50SX Dorchester West–Weymouth appeared in the timetable, most likely with the stock off the morning train. This was, of course, the year Bournemouth line services were decelerated to accommodate temporary speed restrictions for electrification work.

For some years following the end of the 1965 timetable a morning train continued to run between Weymouth and Dorchester South or West, returning in the afternoon approximately at times scholars travelled. They were fully advertised in public timetables with most running on Saturdays as well as Mondays to Fridays. As they would therefore have conveyed both ordinary passengers as well as scholars, I do not consider they come into the remit of this study, so think this is also the appropriate stage to close this article.

Conclusion

While researching in timetables for this article I did notice that Hants & Dorset included works services that may not have operated over bank holidays, etc. A simple note was included warning that such journeys were 'liable to alteration or suspension without notice to the public'. So job done and the public duly warned. In retrospect one wonders if non-advertised trains could have been similarly included in public timetables before they were, and with a similarly worded warning.

Today, with the growth of colleges and universities, many students travel by train to reach them. Doubtless in the future, education methods will change and it will be interesting to see if this brings about an increased use of railways, although the increase in frequency of many services over the years has helped to kill off the 'do not advertise' mentality of former years.

Abbreviations

CLS – Colour light signalling

DEMU – Diesel electric multiple unit

DMMU – Diesel mechanical multiple unit

ECS – Empty coaching stock (empty train)

EDL – Electro-diesel locomotive

EMU – Electric multiple unit

LE – Light engine

P notices – Weekly printed special traffic notices prepared and distributed by divisional offices

P&P – Pull and push train

SN – Daily special notices in addition to P notices typed on stencils at and distributed by divisional offices

SR – Southern Region

WSO – Wednesdays and Saturdays only

WSX – Wednesdays and Saturdays excepted

WTT – Working timetable

WR – Western Region

Sources of Information and Acknowledgement

British Rail Working Timetables

Carriage Working Notices

Southern Railway Public Timetables summer 1939 and winter 1947–48

BR Southern Region Public Timetables thereafter

Bradshaw's British Railways Official Guide & Hotel Directory, January 1948 published by Henry Blacklock & Co Ltd.

London and South Western Railway timetables 7 June to 30 September 1914 or until further notice. Reprinted by Ian Allan Publishing Ltd, 1967.

Hants and Dorset Motor Services Ltd timetable May 1972 until further notice.

An Illustrated History of Southern Pull–Push Stock by Mike King. Published 2006 by Ian Allan Publishing Ltd.

Castleman's Corkscrew Volume 1 by B. L. Jackson. Published 2007 by The Oakwood Press.

Castleman's Corkscrew Volume 2 by B. L. Jackson. Published 2008 by The Oakwood Press.

Operating British Railways History, Southern Region part 3 – Wessex by T. S. Bradshaw. Published by XPress Publications.

Signal Box Register Volume 4 Southern Railway. Edited by C. K. Hall. Published by Signalling Record Society, 2009.

Extracts from the following editions of *The Railway Observer* published by the Railway Correspondence and Travel Society. No 341 July 1957, No 355 September 1958, No 359 January 1959, No 364 June 1959, No 367 September 1959, No 374 April 1960, No 375 May 1960, No 379 September 1960, No 381 November 1960, No 383 January 1961, No 387 May 1961.

And finally my memory, now becoming somewhat frayed around the edges.

Southern Multiple Unit Photography

Alan Postlethwaite

Introduction

There are plenty of good technical photos around of diesel and electric multiple units, often featuring a clean train against a plain background. More challenging, though, are DEMU and EMU photographs of artistic merit that can stir the soul.

This article examines the compositional attempts of three photographers, namely Colin Hogg (*CH*), Alan Postlethwaite (*AFP*) and John J. Smith (*JJS*). The photos date from the 1950s and '60s except for two glass negatives (*GN*) from the 1920s by a Southern Railway photographer. All the photos are available on the Bluebell Railway Photographic Archive website and are copyright protected.

A 6-PUL glides majestically out of Hastings to Victoria. Introduced in 1933 by Maunsell, the gangways of these steel-clad units were inter-car but not inter-unit. The signal bracket dates from the 1931 rebuild of the station.
AFP©Bluebell

Signal Settings

These two SE&CR balanced brackets have arrowhead finials and co-acting arms. They date from 1914 when Bickley Junction was built. The augmented 4-SUB unit is of 1925 vintage. The bow ends are a design feature inherited from the L&SWR 3-SUBs. All the EMUs built until 1932 were conversions of LB&SCR, L&SWR and SE&CR steam stock. This train is signalled to Orpington. Civil work is ongoing to quadruple the line to Swanley and will ease the curves to the SER main line and change the LC&DR track designations from down–down–up–up to down–up–down–up. *AFP©Bluebell*

Opposite: Gallows signals were unusual (although certainly not unique) on the SR. At Sutton, two tall LB&SCR brackets with SR arms frame a Bulleid 4-SUB unit, which is signalled for Mitcham Junction. The Epsom Downs branch joins from the right at a maximum speed of 20mph. *AFP©Bluebell*

People Settings

In each photo, passengers or railwaymen transform the scene from a technical record into a composition with a story.

Unlike the commotion of London's last tram, passengers barely outnumber staff for the very last overhead electric departure from Victoria in 1928. Does anyone know to what the EFB sign refers? 'Electric Formation Brake' perhaps? *JJS-GN©Bluebell*

A busy scene at London Bridge on 1 December 1968 as passengers board the Brighton Belle. The train's regular terminus, Victoria, was inaccessible due to engineering work at Battersea. Concourse photos are quite rare and yet they can capture the busy atmosphere of a major terminus. London Bridge had twenty-one platforms. *JJS©Bluebell*

A quiet scene at Reigate showing the rugged front detail of a 2-BIL cab. These Maunsell units were introduced in 1935 with steel-clad wooden bodies. *AFP©Bluebell*

Sorting the parcels and saying goodbye at Portsmouth and Southsea. High Level. Introduced in 1937, the Maunsell 4-CORs were also steel-clad and were the first with inter-unit gangways. Their blind eye earned the nickname 'Nelsons'. *AFP©Bluebell*

Below: A Hastings DEMU draws into Sevenoaks as a young couple prepare to board for a sunny day out by the sea. *AFP*

Station Settings

The 2-SL units were 1928 rebuilds of LB&SCR overhead electric driving cars. They were given standard SR cab ends but retained the low flat roof where the pantograph once was. They served only the South London line. The first picture is at Wandsworth Road. The second picture is at South Bermondsey. The plain wooden island platform was built by the SR in place of the centre track, which was originally used for empty stock working from Peckham Rye. Such elevated stations tended to be spartan, draughty and also eerie at night. *JJS ©Bluebell*

These Bulleid units were the SR's first all-steel 4-SUBs, the first to include semi-saloons and the first with flat ends. Unit 4127 is at Holmwood (hardly 'SUBurban'!), framed by the over-track booking office, footbridge and LB&SCR signal box. Unit 4120 is at East Dulwich, framed by signals, cables, a fogman's hut and signal box. *AFP©Bluebell*

Gas holders, cooling towers, sidings and a wooden shelter frame a 2-WIM unit at Waddon Marsh halt. *JJS©Bluebell*

A mass of station detail at Wadhurst, glistening in the rain. The DEMU and figures bring the scene to life. The signal box is of Dutton manufacture, while the station building was designed by William Tress. *AFP©Bluebell*

A balanced composition at Beddington Lane Halt with a 2-WIM unit. These trains were originally LB&SCR bogie steam stock. They were converted to overhead electric trailers, then converted back to steam stock and were finally reconverted in 1929 to become outside-third EMUs for the Wimbledon–West Croydon line. *JJS©Bluebell*

A simple composition at Bexhill Central with a 2-HAL train approaching from Eastbourne. These all-steel units were introduced by Bulleid in 1937 for outer suburban duties. *AFP©Bluebell*

The wooden running-in board and a tall overhanging signal box frame a 4-LAV unit at Gatwick Racecourse. These steel-clad wooden units were introduced by Maunsell in 1932 for semi-fast duties. *JJS©Bluebell*

Rural Settings

Framed by a great telegraph pole, a dramatic up shot of the Brighton Belle near Purley Oaks. *CH@©Bluebell*

Winter birch and the south portal of Somerhill tunnel frame a DEMU en route to Hastings. *AFP©Bluebell*

Willows, shadow and an SR handed bracket frame a 2-BIL unit approaching Lewes from Brighton. *AFP©Bluebell*

Multiple Trains

Ancient and modern at Waterloo but it is the electric 4-COR unit that is the older. This was built in the late 1930s whereas the class Q1 alongside was to a 1942 design. The composition is well balanced with excellent sunlight and shadow. *AFP©Bluebell*

Southwark Cathedral provides a perfect backdrop on the western approach to London Bridge. The EPB services are Charing Cross to Addiscombe (headcode 36) and Cannon Street to Dartford via Blackheath and Charlton (headcode 61). *AFP©Bluebell*

The glorious Weald of Kent as seen from above the south portal of Weald tunnel. The purpose of the outing was to photograph the last vestiges of SER steam but a Hastings DEMU poked its nose out at just the right moment to create this juxtaposition of motive power. The locomotive is Battle of Britain class Pacific No 34070 *Manston*. *AFP©Bluebell*

With eleven tracks and four EMUs on the London Bridge approach, the London & Greenwich line has expanded somewhat. The tracks (L to R) are: South London lines (3); Brighton main lines (3); and five South Eastern lines (two up and three down). Eight have outside-third electrification while the South London overhead catenary is in its final year (1928). The SR subsequently changed the South London RH track designation to become the Brighton up Local. *JJS-GN*

Peripheral interest at West Croydon includes the Wimbledon bay, the RH passenger ramp, a handed signal bracket and the up line with single slip point. The units are a 2-WIM and a 4-SUB. *JJS©Bluebell*

Time for a chat at Dartford between station staff and the EPB crew. Two halves always make a whole! *AFP©Bluebell*

Two disparate diesel units terminating at Portsmouth and Southsea low-level. Western Region, with mechanical drive on the left, and Southern Region, with electric drive on the right and its bland EPB-type cab end. The WR set will have arrived from Reading while headcode 67 is for a Southern region train from either Salisbury or Andover Junction. The dominant central interest is provided by scattered barrows, parcels and the post-war canopy. *AFP©Bluebell*

Postscript – Riding the Multiple Units

My earliest memory is as a 6-year-old being bundled into the ladies only compartment of a wooden EMU 'for safe keeping'. It made me feel like a prince. Living at Catford, we invariably used the SER line to town, the elevated LC&DR station was somehow alien and served only the bombed out City. I also recall that I did once travel down the Catford Loop to a Cub camp near Tonbridge. A novelty was to change trains at Sevenoaks with a choice of platforms to either side.

During my engineering apprenticeship, I commuted to London Bridge from Catford Bridge and later, after we moved house, from East Dulwich. I liked to lean out of the carriage window on the racetrack down to New Cross. I explored every corner of London Bridge station and stood in awe as train after train came through, destined for unknown suburbs such as Sanderstead, Bromley North and Dartford loop. Then an announcement would blare – 'stand well back on platform 3 – and a hot steam train would come thundering through to goodness knows where. At 5.07 each evening, there were simultaneous departures for the Mid Kent line – fast to Ladywell from platform 1 – and fast to Catford Bridge from platform 3. Ten minutes later, a similar duo departed.

While studying at Northampton College, I had two winters in lodgings at Streatham, commuting to Holborn Viaduct via Herne Hill and walking up through Smithfield to Islington. It was a pleasant, interesting journey, full of history and with few delays. I remember the red, yellow and silver vans of the *Star*, *News* and *Standard* lined up by the antiquated Holborn platforms to transfer newspapers on to the evening commuter trains.

My longest distance commute was for two years between Meopham and Blackfriars, then walking through the deep, dark, dank subway beneath Blackfriars Bridge goods station. Despite its history, the fascination of the L&CDR soon faded as the journey became monotonous. Delays were frequent in those days, while the buffet at Swanley was useful while waiting for a delayed train. Then BR closed the buffet and instead made us change at Farningham Road, which had no proper shelter from the elements. Blackfriars, too, was a notoriously draughty station.

After my parents moved to Hastings, I used to visit them by as many different routes as possible. The LB&SCR route was comfortable but I always resented the time wasted going in and out of Eastbourne. I preferred the more direct SER route via Tonbridge in a plush new DEMU with buffet car and enjoyed the glorious Rowland Hilder scenery of the High Weald. Occasionally I took a steam train down the long LC&DR line to Ashford and then the little DEMU via Rye. Best of all was to pick up a vintage steam train at Eastbourne for a slow ride up the Cuckoo line via Horam and then Oxted. So, yes, I have to admit that I am primarily a devotee of steam. The EMUs and DEMUs are, shall we say, an additional interest.

I escaped London when my work transferred to Tilbury and I commuted on the Gravesend ferry. Then we moved to the Cotswolds, where I commuted by car in princely comfort to Gloucester. I know people who did the London commute for a lifetime. Some were also in-and-outers, one living in Maidstone to work in Croydon and another living in Southend-on-Sea to work in Leatherhead. I did it myself for a short while between Clapham and Belvedere.

Why do we commute? The Romans founded Londinium as a military and administrative stronghold. It grew into a major commercial and cultural centre and eventually became the constitutional capital. The city was nourished by shops and market gardens beyond its walls. Freight was carried mainly on the Thames and then on the canals, especially the Grand Union. Finally, the industrial revolution brought railways and industries to the London area, accompanied by a population explosion that turned myriad villages into suburbs. Central London was the major employer and rail the main carrier.

The railway tentacles of London spread all along the south coast, and indeed throughout the Home Counties. The rituals of commuting have been satirised beautifully by Tony Hancock on film and by Leonard Rossiter on TV with no one ever talking and everyone doing exactly the same each day. Spike Milligan once rode a commuter train in pink mohair trousers and no one batted an eyelid. Tens of millions commute willingly into cities worldwide, although to do so in the same style of pink trousers is not compulsory.

So what were the personalities of the SR multiple units? With its smart livery and well-ironed sides, the *Brighton Belle* was clearly the aristocrat, although I never rode it. The PULs and PANs were comfortably middle class, with square spectacles and a bowler hat over the cab. The vee-nose South Western SUBs were the inquisitive clerical classes. The BILs were country runabouts with whiskers adorning the cab front. The CORs were the rough-and-tumblers whose noses had been broken in a fight. And the WIMs and SLs were the working class hand-me-downs that looked as though they had been squashed by a steam roller. The happiest faces were the Bulleid SUBs, with round-cornered windows and bulging bellies. Hastings DEMUs, on the other hand, had a sad, narrow look and could be very noisy. Distinctive personalities were everywhere until usurped by the bland EPBs, CEPs and the like. Those were the days!

Why are the station names repeated? And what was the attraction of Thames Ditton for 163 Catfordians?

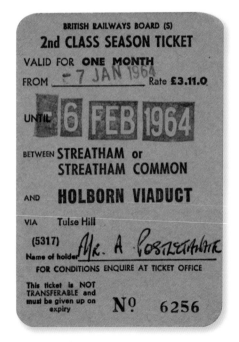

Permanent Way Trolleys

Jeremy Staines

A recent acquisition has been a file of papers appertaining to the use of motor trolleys, starting with the Elham Valley line in 1930. Never as prolific in their use as on the Great Western, the Southern Railway and its successor the Southern Region would, however, use motor trolleys on certain sections of line for some decades. The final variant was the well-known 'Wickham' version, examples of which may still be seen on heritage railways today.

Why the Southern Railway should have been interested in trolleys in the first place is a simply matter of economics. Up to around 1930 the various permanent way gangs would be stationed around the system, usually under the control of a ganger. This man (and his men) were responsible for everyday maintenance of the track over a set distance. The number of men in the gang and the distance of responsibility were variable according to the number of lines and frequency of traffic. In addition, the ganger, or his assistant, the sub-ganger, was required to patrol the length daily carrying a large hammer. (On double track lines the practice was usually to walk 'facing' the traffic). He would look out for keys that had come loose, knocking these back into place as well as observing for any signs of other defects – sleepers that needed packing underneath, etc. His men, the gang, would then be detailed to the work site to carry out any necessary maintenance. Permanent way, sometimes referred to as 'ganger's huts', were located at intervals along the section and were where tools and equipment were stored as well as providing a location where respite might be taken. The gang would also undertake the necessary trimming back and mowing of grass on cutting sides and embankments as well as lopping branches and clearing culverts and drains when needed. More major work, relaying, etc, would be the responsibility of a 'relaxing gang', although invariably assisted by the local gang. One final task the men undertook was that of acting as 'fogmen' when required.

It follows that this was both a labour intensive and time-consuming operation. While mechanisation as it exists today in the form of ro-rail machines and cranes was well into the future (excepting of course the permanent way department cranes used for relaying when required), the Southern Railway was well aware of the savings made, particularly by the GWR in reducing gang numbers and at the same time increasing its respective area of responsibility by the simple expedient of providing mechanised transport. By this means two objectives were achieved. The first was that the gang could be conveyed to their place of work, so saving on walking time. (This was a major consideration, for say as an example the site of work was two miles from the gang home station, this would entail a two-hour walk at the start and end of the day and mean perhaps only half the actual working day was available for work. The ganger, too, could inspect his length from a motor car, although to ensure nothing was missed he was still expected to 'walk the length' at least once weekly.) While the Southern would eventually use a considerable number of motor trolleys for gang and material transport, its use of individual inspection trolleys was small compared with say the GWR.

Lengthmen riding to work in a Wickham trolley neat Teston Halt (Maidstone) in 1934. The trolley will have been signalled with a special bell code between the departing and next signal box, and with the 'driver' required to obey all fixed signals. Owing to their light weight, trolleys could not always be expected to activate track circuits, while they were also liable to derail and catch at spring-loaded catch/trap points. *R. W. Kidner*

At this point the reader may well ask the obvious question, 'Why might the gang not be carried to and dropped off at their site of work by a train, passenger or goods, travelling in the same direction?' The answer is they may well have been – but only on occasions. Sometimes the service was inconvenient, while on certain lines it was impractical to stop the service mid-section.

The bottom line in all of this was one word, 'economy'. Savings could, and were achieved, although it must be said sometimes at the expense of lost jobs or men having to seek railway employment some distance from their original location. As was common at the time, the human cost is not referred to in the file.

Up to 1930, such trolleys as were available were invariably of the hand-propelled type. Certainly they were in use, but their sphere of activity was limited. Should a trolley also be put on the line, the section was then 'blocked' until a member of the gang had returned to the signal box to confirm it had been removed and the section clear again for the passage of

trains. Technology would now change both of these aspects; the application of the internal combustion engine applied to a trolley and the use of the 'occupation key' system, meaning a trolley could travel into a section and the section then be restored when the trolley was removed from the track and the occupation key restored to a special instrument. To be fair, both these technologies had been available for some time in various forms, the occupation key system especially having been in use on the GWR since the earliest years of the twentieth century.

So, to return to the involvement of the Southern Railway and where the available papers (but perhaps not necessarily the story) commence at the Divisional Superintendent's Office, London Bridge, on 10 October 1930. In a letter from an unnamed individual sent to F. Bushrod at Waterloo headed 'Canterbury South – signalling of power-worked trolley' it refers to a petrol trolley recently introduced for maintenance on the Elham Valley line. 'This trolley is stationed at Canterbury South and starts away at about 7.45 am and returns there at

A series of three publicity images (the originals slightly retouched in places) showing the process of removing (and replacing) a trolley on the track. A small hand turntable was carried on the trolley that would be placed between the rails adjacent to the trolley run-off point. Although the views depict just two men being involved, in practice a trolley of this size would require four – hence the lifting bar running across the front and rear. The location (or railway company) is not given. The principal manufacturer of these products as used in the UK were Messrs Wickham of Ware in Hertfordshire, although Messrs Buda from the USA were also active in promoting their own products. The manufacturer of this particular railcar is not confirmed although it is very likely to have been an early Wickham. Motor trolleys delivered to the SR were given a DS series, followed by what is believed to have been a two-digit number. This in itself implies there were perhaps not all that number in total. In BR(S) days the identification changed to 'DS3xxx'. The Wickham Works List, referred to in the acknowledgements, gives some information as to where new trolleys were allocated, and this is appended as Appendix A.

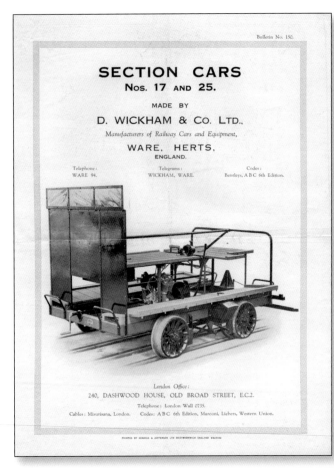

5.30 pm. As in accordance with Block Regulation 9A, a power-worked trolley can only be put on or taken off the line at a block-post, it means that Canterbury South Box has to open for the purpose. This, in effect, is costing us one Porter/Signalman at £117 per annum, whereas if some dispensation could be given whereby the Ganger were allowed to telephone Harpledown Junction Box for permission to put the trolley on the line and to intimate that it has been taken off, the Porter/Signalman in question could be retrenched.' *(What a lovely use of words – Ed!)*

The letter continues, 'In view of the scarcity of traffic over this line, I feel that such relaxation would be attended by very little risk and perhaps you would give the matter favourable consideration. To enable the Ganger to use the telephone at Canterbury South it would be necessary to supply him with a key of the Signal box there.'

The whole point of using a motorised trolley was in itself to save on costs. One man, or gang, was able to cover greater distances both for inspection purposes and also when it was necessary to travel to a site of work. Consequently, it is perhaps slightly surprising that the subject continued to be discussed for several months apparently without a decision being reached.

Publicity images for the Wickham type petrol railcar and trailer. Compared with the earlier views, any protection against the elements was still rudimentary. Notice the lifting handles referred to and the starting handle. As will be gathered also from the accompanying description, the fuel used was petrol.

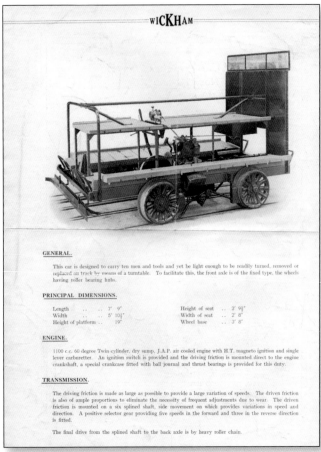

Above: This particular model was intended for the ganger alone, although a passenger might also be carried. The Southern Railway appeared to make little use of this type of vehicle but even so it would be dangerous to say 'never'. Note the reference to a 'Sturmey–Archer' gearbox, a name that will be familiar to those of a certain age who had a bicycle in their youth. The final development of this type of trolley saw a curved bonnet provided together with a windscreen and a hood. Such vehicles would then continue to work well into BR days, also being painted in BR 'maroon and cream' livery.

Above right and right: The Buda design vehicle, which provided no protection whatsoever to any member of the crew. Certainly in later years Wickham at least began to provide enclosed sides and ends to all its trolleys, while on the GWR (presumably also on the Southern) a cover might have been made and fitted unofficially. Trolleys such as these were in use for maintenance on railways throughout the world.

Then, in February 1931, it was noted that the trolley would now work through to Harpledon Junction, although it was pointed out that if the Elham Valley line was converted to a single track as was then being discussed separately, 'will be quite impossible to work the branch with motor trolleys unless some means of removing them from the rails at intermediate points, such as provided by the Great Western Economic System, is installed, and failing this it will be necessary to revert to the old system of length gangs which will prevent any appreciable saving in manpower made on the conversion to a single line.'

The eventual outcome was that the Southern Railway was not prepared to issue the ganger with a key to Canterbury South Signal Box, where he might obtain verbal authorisation to occupy the line from the man at Harpledon Junction, and instead approved expenditure of £10 for the removal of the 'garage' (used to store the trolley) from Canterbury South to Harpledon Junction itself.

A trolley shed, complete with its run-off point, the trolley itself and associated trailer recorded at Wickham (Meon Valley line). *Denis Callender*

While this matter was still being discussed on the Eastern Section, on 10 December 1930 the Central division was suggesting that maintenance costs on the Hawkhurst and Lydd branches could also be reduced by again using power trolleys. This was approved and the trolleys were ordered (we do not know at this stage what type). As a matter of subsidiary interest, we may wonder why the matter was being discussed by the Central division as surely neither branch was ever in its 'parish'?

Meanwhile, Waterloo recognised that this was an opportunity for effecting savings on a number of lines across the railway with mention made that, 'Schemes involving the use of trollies (sic) are in preparation for the sections Barnstaple Junction to Torrington and Halwill Junction to Bude.'

Waterloo was concerned though that before embarking on a programme 'of such magnitude ...' rules for the operating of trolleys covering both single and double lines should be drawn up and a committee formed with representatives from all the relevant departments. It was noted that even at this early stage is was essential that pathways for trolley working be available in both the morning and evening, '... such that the men can be got to their work without delay and back again without payment of overtime.'

Matters now appear to move fast as a meeting was held at Waterloo on 17 February 1931 with representatives from the S & T, engineering and traffic departments. It was quickly agreed that in most cases a trolley could be put on and taken off a single line route at a 'token' station (meaning the place where the token/staff/tablet would be issued to the driver so he might enter the single line section), although it was also recognised that in a few cases it may be desirable to have an intermediate occupation key instrument and telephone. This latter facility would be necessary where the men might need

It is a matter of regret that it has not been possible to locate an image for publication of trolley working on any of the Kent branches mentioned. Brian Hart, in his excellent history *Elham Valley Line* (Wild Swan Publications 1984), does though show a Buda trolley at Bridge station on p28. On the rear cover of *The Hawkhurst Branch* by the same author and publisher (2000), a run-off point for the trolley at the end of the platform at Hawkhurst may also be seen. On 2 May 1931 formal instructions for trolley working were issued to cover the Hawkhurst line as well as trolley working between Lydd, New Romney, Dungeness and Appledore. Here a later Wickham trolley and trailer are viewed near Binegar on the Somerset & Dorset line. Motor trolley use on this line had been extant prior to the Second World War. *R. E. Toop*

SOUTHERN RAILWAY

Instruction No. 14a, 1932.

General Instructions respecting the use of
POWER WORKED TROLLEYS
and
POWER WORKED TROLLEYS WITH TRAILER
by Engineer's Department.

1. POWER WORKED TROLLEYS (OR TRAILERS WHEN USED IN CONNECTION WITH SUCH TROLLEYS) MUST NOT BE PLACED UPON ANY RUNNING LINE UNTIL THE PERMISSION OF THE SIGNALMAN HAS BEEN OBTAINED and, except as provided in Clause 10 of these instructions, must only be placed upon or removed from the lines at a signal box.

2. When upon the line a power worked trolley must be treated as a train, and a head lamp which must show a white light during darkness, fog, or falling snow, must be carried in front and a tail lamp which must show a red light during darkness, fog, or falling snow, must be carried at the rear. If a trailer is attached the tail lamp must be carried at the rear of the trailer and care must be taken that neither the head lamp nor the tail lamp is obscured by men or materials carried on the trolley or trailer.

3. Not more than one trailer (loaded or empty) must be attached to a power worked trolley.

4. When a power worked trolley is required to haul a trailer the man in charge must satisfy himself that the extra coupling provided is brought into use and arrange for a competent man to travel on the trailer in order to apply the brake when necessary.

5. Except on those sections of the line where occupation keys are in use, and in regard to which special instructions are issued, power worked trolleys must be signalled in accordance with Block Regulation No. 9A.

6. Except in the case of power worked trolleys detained at home signals on single lines when the man in charge is in possession of a tablet, staff, key token, or occupation key, as the case may be, the provisions of Rule 55 must be observed in all cases where such trolleys are detained at signals, and a competent man must be sent to the signal box to remind the Signalman of the position of the trolley. Should the Driver be unaccompanied by any other member of the staff he must see that the trolley is properly secured before leaving it for the purpose of proceeding to the signal box.

7. Track Circuits or Treadles must not be relied upon for the protection of power worked trolleys.

8. In the event of a power worked trolley being stopped by accident, failure, obstruction or other exceptional cause, and it is not possible at once to remove it from the rails, the man in charge must arrange for the obstruction to be immediately protected in accordance with Rules 217a, 218 and 219. Should the Driver be unaccompanied by any other member of the staff he must himself proceed to carry out the requirements of these Rules and in the event of the line used by trains running in the opposite direction being obstructed he must arrange for the protection of the opposite line before proceeding to protect the obstruction from the rear.

9. When it is necessary for a power worked trolley to remain stationary on the line for more than three minutes, other than detentions at signals (for which see paragraph 6) the man in charge must, unless he is in possession of the tablet, staff, key token, or occupation key, arrange for the trolley to be protected in accordance with the Rule 251.

10. (a) Except where special instructions are issued to the contrary, a power worked trolley, or power worked trolley with a trailer attached, when being worked on a single line may return to the signal box in the rear provided the man in charge is in possession of the tablet, staff, key token, or occupation key, AND HAS OBTAINED THE PERMISSION OF THE SIGNALMAN IN THE REAR TO DO SO.

(b) A power worked trolley may be removed from the single line before reaching the next signal box, and if such a course is intended and no further occupation of the single line is required before the passage of the next train, prior arrangements must be made with the Signalman before the power worked trolley enters the section. When, in such a case, the trolley is removed from the line, the man in charge must, except where occupation keys are in use, send a competent man with the tablet, staff, or key token, as the case may be, to the signal box at the end of the section, in accordance with the arrangements already made. The Signalman, on receiving the tablet, staff, or key token and on being informed that the power worked trolley (or power worked trolley and trailer) is clear of the line, must send the "Train out of Section" or "Cancelling" signal, as the case may be.

(c) A power worked trolley may be placed on a single line away from a signal box. Should this course be necessary the man in charge must, except where occupation keys are in use, first send a competent man to the signal box at the most convenient end of the section and obtain from the Signalman there a tablet, staff, or key token, and the Signalman must, before handing the tablet, staff, or key token to this man, pull and replace the signal leading into the section to be occupied so as to restore the locking on this signal. The power worked trolley must be signalled to the box at the other end of the section about to be occupied and when it reaches either that box or the box from which the tablet, staff, or key token was obtained or alternatively is removed from the single line and the tablet, staff, or key token has been delivered to the Signalman, the "Train out of Section" or "Cancelling" signal, as the case may be, must be sent.

Note :—*On tablet sections where non-returnable instruments are in use, the man in charge must take into consideration the fact that if the trolley is required to proceed to the box from which the tablet is drawn it will afterwards be necessary for the tablet to be conveyed to the other end of the section.*

(d) Until the man returns to the power worked trolley with the tablet, staff, or key token, neither a power worked trolley nor a trailer which is to be used in connection with such power worked trolley must be placed on the single line.

11. A portable turntable is provided with each power worked trolley to enable the power worked trolley or trailer to be expeditiously placed upon and removed from the rails and this turntable must always be carried on the power worked trolley.

12. No man must be allowed to sit on the front of a trailer or on the back of a power worked trolley when a trailer is attached thereto.

13. A power worked trolley, or power worked trolley drawing a trailer, must not be allowed to exceed a speed of thirty miles per hour and the motor must be kept in gear when running down steep gradients. When running out of gear the vehicle must be kept under complete control. Stations, signal boxes and catch points must be approached with care. When a power worked trolley is propelling a trailer, the speed must not exceed six miles per hour.

14. Each power worked trolley when upon the line must carry at least two red flags, two green flags, two hand lamps, not less than 12 detonators, a fire extinguisher and a Klaxon horn.

15. The man in charge will be held responsible for seeing that the foregoing instructions are carried out. No person may drive a power worked trolley unless he has been examined jointly and certified as competent by the Permanent Way Inspector and District Traffic Inspector, and has been duly authorised by his Divisional Engineer to act as trolley driver.

Each authorised driver of a power worked trolley will be issued with a copy of Extracts from Block Regulations, etc., which came into operation on the 2nd February, 1930.

16. When a trailer is used independently of a power worked trolley it must be treated as an ordinary trolley and the provisions of Rules 246, 247, 248, 249 and 250 will apply.

BY ORDER.

WATERLOO STATION,
October, 1932.

(Eng. Mis/16,428)
(S. of O. R.47,968).

Formal (general) instructions for motor, or as referred to by the SR, power worked trolleys.

to work 'mid-section' while also removing the trolley from the line to enable ordinary traffic to pass. The costs was estimated at £150 for a key box three miles from the controlling token point and £15 per mile thereafter (how these figures were arrived at is not stated). The meeting also agreed what was perhaps obvious, that if expenditure were required this would have to be considered against the likely saving to be made should trolleys be introduced.

Here we should explain exactly what 'occupation key' working was, compared with conventional working. In the case of the latter, the driver of a train cannot enter a section of line (and for convenience we will refer to a single line), without having in his possession the appropriate tablet/staff/token. The release of this precludes another being obtained until the first has been restored to the signalling instrument at the other end of the section. If a trolley were going through the complete section then the ganger must also have 'token'

(generic word), and, of course, no train may enter at either end of the section until the trolley has passed through and the token is restored.

Should the ganger wish to stop mid-section then he may, of course, do so but all the while no other train may enter the section.

Occupation key working was a more flexible means of operating. Instead of a 'token', the ganger took possession of an 'occupation key'. As with the 'token', this could only be obtained with the consent of the signalmen at either end of the section *and* provided no staff/tablet/token had already been released. The release of the occupation key electrically locked the 'token' system, which could not be restored until the occupation key was itself restored. The flexibility now possible was that the occupation key could be restored at an intermediate occupation key box – the trolley, of course, first being removed from the running line! With both of these done, the section of line might

Regrettably no images of the actual keys used on any of the branches have come to light, and indeed the SR keys themselves appear to be conspicuous by their absence on the railwayman circuit. We can therefore only illustrate a key from the 'opposition', the GWR, this one being a blank without engraving. The GWR keys were one of at least six configurations, the idea being the same as that for a token/staff/tablet in that a key would only fit the instruments on a particular section of line and could then be carried over.

have a train pass by, after which the ganger (and his men) could continue their work once they had again obtained the key from the intermediate box – once more with the consent of the signalmen, of course. Hence, a telephone was also provided at each intermediate occupation key box. Unlike with staff/tablet/token working where several 'tokens' were provided although only one might be released at any one time – to allow several trains to follow in the same direction if necessary – there was only ever one occupation key per section.

Notwithstanding the date the working instructions were issued for the Hawkhurst, Lydd, New Romney, Dungeness and Appledore lines, it is perhaps surprising that up to now there is no mention of the involvement of the Ministry of Transport, which would have to be notified when an alteration of working was envisaged on any line carrying passenger traffic. (New works or the method of working over a passenger carrying line, which this did, had to be sanctioned by the Ministry of Transport. Sometimes it was a 'rubber stamp' job, but in cases where a variation was required then, while approval to commence might well be given, a physical inspection would follow later.) Indeed, the first reference appears in a letter from the Ministry of Transport to Waterloo dated 27 July 1931 and refers to a letter

Formal drawings of the face for the key and switch boxes. From these we learn of the manufacturer and that the system used was almost identical to that of the GWR. (To obtain the key, which would normally be locked in the slot shown, the ganger must first obtain the verbal permission of the signalman, who would in turn communicate the request to the signalman at the opposite end of the section. With both men in agreement, the ganger would turn the key to position '3' and await the flag 'Free' to be shown, at which point the key could be withdrawn. The token instruments would now be locked at either end of the section.) Restoration of the key was a simple 'insert and turn' procedure.)

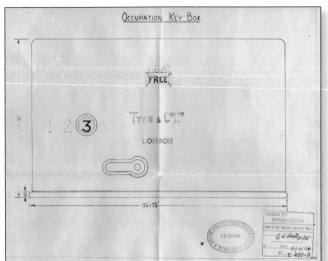

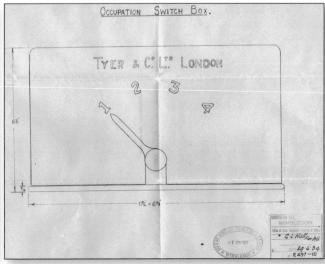

sent from the SR to the ministry dated one week earlier. This letter approves new works in connection with motor trolley use between Launceston and Halwill. A note in the file dated 10 December 1931 also states that the actual trolleys had now arrived on site and, '... it is proposed, therefore, to use these instead of light engines for testing purposes.'

Of particular interest is Point 9, referring to the occupation key boxes having 'spring locks and handles'. Whether this had come about due to some incident or other is not reported but certainly by June 1932 it was agreed that the key boxes would be secured using carriage door locks. (This had not been found necessary on the Elham Valley line installation and where the key boxes were either in a signal box or station office.) In consequence, a revised formal notice, 'No 10a (1932)' to cover the operation of the section between Ashwater and Launceston by the engineer's department was issued.

Formal approval of the Ashwater and Launceston working was given by Col A. C. Trench for the Ministry of Transport on 28 June 1934, which followed his site inspection of 15 June. (It

was noted that his colleague, Col A. H. L. Mount, had originally been detailed to undertake the inspection.)

Meanwhile, in February 1931 and accepted as being a little out of chronological order, the file refers to the possible use of a trolley to run from Basingstoke to Alton leaving in the morning and returning in the late afternoon. Revenue accrued from the B & A line was already sparse, the limited service designed around using just one train crew not incurring overtime. As such, the last train from Alton to Basingstoke departed as early as 4.20pm and with the single line section extending the whole 13 miles with no intermediate block post, the only option available was to retime the train – something unacceptable to the traffic department – or incurring overtime. With neither option considered acceptable the Basingstoke and Alton railway would never see motor trolley working. (No doubt an investment of £150+ for an intermediate key box was similarly not considered worthwhile, although this is not mentioned in the correspondence.) In the event the railway was already on borrowed time as formal closure took place on 12 September 1932.

Below and overleaf: Working instructions for the Mid Hants and Meon Valley lines. This was the fourth form of economy measures on these and associated routes in just over a decade. The first had been the closure of the signal box and removal the passing loop at Privett on the MV line. Then, in 1931 the crossing loops and signal boxes were taken out of use at Itchen Abbas and Ropley on the MH line. Next, in 1932 the Basingstoke and Alton had closed and with it Butts Junction signal box located at the configuration of the B & A, MH and MV lines just west of Alton. Finally, in 1933 trolley working was introduced on the two surviving lines. It should be mentioned that it is not clear how long such an arrangement lasted on the Mid Hants; certainly so far as the Meon valley was concerned, trolleys were in use until closure in 1955.

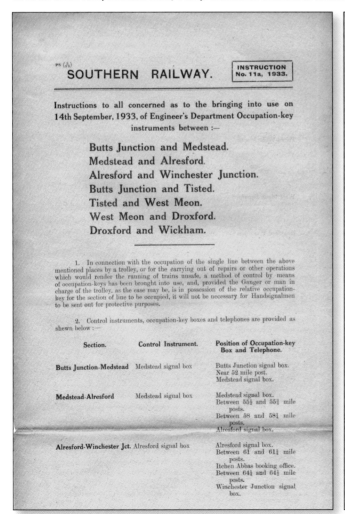

3

When an occupation-key has been replaced in an occupation-key box by the Ganger or man in charge of the trolley, he must remain at the telephone until this test has been made and he has been informed by the Signalman at the control signal box that the tablet instruments are again in order. He must then replace the telephone receiver, and close and lock the cupboard containing the occupation-key box.

Should it be found that the restoration of the key at an intermediate occupation-key box fails to establish tablet working, or in the event of the key having been damaged so that it cannot be replaced in the instrument, the Ganger or man in charge of the trolley must be instructed by the Signalman at the control signal box to take the key by means of the motor trolley as quickly as possible to the nearest signal box. Upon arrival at that box the Signalman must, if practicable, place the key in the occupation-key box in accordance with the instructions contained in the first two paragraphs of this clause. If the restoration of the occupation-key in the occupation-key box at the signal box concerned fails to establish tablet working, or in the event of it not being possible to place the occupation-key in the occupation-key box at the signal box concerned, the Pilotman must take possession of the occupation-key and, if necessary, may use the Petrol trolley for the purpose of establishing working by Pilotman. The Pilotman must keep the occupation-key in his possession until it is required to be taken away by the Lineman or until the tablet apparatus is again repaired and ready for use.

5. Under no circumstances must an occupation-key be placed in any of the occupation-key boxes until the line is clear and safe for the passage of trains.

6. Each occupation-key has lettered upon it the names of the places between which it is available and it must not under any circumstances be carried beyond those places.

7. Before an occupation-key is released, the Signalmen must first agree with each other by telephone whether the occupation may be granted or not; if it be decided that the occupation of the line may be permitted, the Ganger or man in charge of the trolley must be clearly informed by the Signalman the exact times between which the occupation is authorised and in deciding these times it must be arranged for the occupation to cease 10 minutes before a train is due to enter the single line. If it be decided that the occupation asked for cannot be allowed, the Ganger or man in charge of the trolley must be so informed.

8. When an occupation-key is required by the Ganger or man in charge of the trolley at a signal box application must be made to the Signalman, who will, if the conditions permit of the occupation being granted, obtain the key by the method laid down in Clause 3.

9. When an occupation-key is required to be withdrawn at any of the intermediate occupation-key boxes, the Ganger or man in charge of the trolley must first get in touch with the Signalman at the control station, and state clearly the following :—

(a) Situation of occupation-key box from which message is being sent.
(b) Length of time for which occupation is required.
(c) Points between which it is intended to carry out work.
(d) If occupation is required for trolleying, the point to which the trolley will be run.

Care must be taken not to turn the occupation-key in any of the occupation-key boxes until an advice has been received from the Signalman that occupation of the line can be permitted.

4

10. The Ganger, when he has obtained occupation of the line for repairs or other operations, will be responsible for the safe custody of the occupation-key during the time of occupation, and he must so arrange his work as to be able to put back the occupation-key at the appointed time.

Should occupation be given up at a signal box, the occupation-key must be handed to the Signalman who will, after communicating by telephone, with the Signalman at the other end of the section, restore the occupation-key in the manner described in Clause 4.

11. In the event of it being necessary to work a section by Pilotman, the Pilotman, when distributing the pilot working forms, must, unless the occupation-key is in his possession, satisfy himself by personal observation that the occupation-key is in one of the occupation-key boxes. In order that he may do this, duplicate keys of the cupboards containing the occupation-key instruments are kept by the Signalmen concerned.

12. The Signalmen must record in their train register books full particulars respecting all applications for occupation of the line.

13. It will only be possible, subject to traffic requirements, for occupation of sections of the line to be obtained when the signal boxes are open, and it must be clearly understood by all concerned that should it be necessary to place a trolley on the line or to perform work which would render the running of trains unsafe at a time when, for any reason, an occupation-key for the section to be occupied cannot be withdrawn, or the Ganger is not in possession of the tablet, such occupation must be carried out strictly in accordance with Rules 215 and 217 and Handsignalmen posted accordingly.

14. The requirements of Regulation No. 9A of the Electric Train Tablet regulations are hereby cancelled in connection with the working of power worked trolleys, provided the man in charge of the trolley is in possession of the relative occupation-key.

15. The provisions laid down in the first portion of Rule 215a, viz. that a trolley must only be placed on the line when the Ganger or man in charge is present, will not apply in so far as the operation of trolleys under the occupation-key system is concerned.

16. Where the word "Ganger" is used in these instructions it includes the Sub-Ganger or other man appointed by the Ganger.

BY ORDER.

WATERLOO STATION,
4th September, 1933.

Eng. Mis. 16,428.
S. of O. R.47,968.

By June 1935 the system had been extended to cover two other lines, namely the Meon Valley and Mid Hants railways. A listing from that time giving details on both these and the other installations already mentioned.

Engineer's Occupation Keys

Power worked trollies had originally been intended to be introduced on the Mid Hants and Meon Valley lines on 13 April 1933 but for reasons that are not stated this was delayed until 14 September.

As mentioned previously, without doubt the Great Western had invested and developed occupation key working more than any of the other railway companies, although the LNER was probably a close second. The GWR, for example, effected economies from the turn of the twentieth century by pioneering the use of pump trolleys coupled with occupation key working to reduce expenditure on a number of branch lines. The advent of the motor trolley would see the concept developed still further on the GWR and it is therefore not surprising to find several references and indeed examples of GWR working on various routes included within the Southern Railway file.

Section and position of Control Instrument:	Occupation key boxes at:	System of block working in force
Alton and Medstead		
Medstead signal box	Alton	Electric train tablet system (Tyer's No 6)
	Butts Junction	
	Near 52 m.p.*	*In all cases where an intermediate key box was provided this also corresponded with a run-off point for the motor trolley. The trolley being manhandled off the rails by the gang.
	Medstead	

Section and position of Control Instrument:	Occupation key boxes at:	System of block working in force
Medstead & Alresford	Medstead box	Electric train tablet system (Tyer's No 3)
	Between 55½ and 55¾ m.p.	
	Between 58 and 58¼ m.p.	
	Alresford Box	
Alresford & Winchester Junc.	Alresford Box	Electric train tablet system (Tyer's No 3)
Alresford signal box	Between 61 and 61¼ m.p.	
	Itchen Abbas box	
	Between 64¼ and 64½ m.p.	
	Winchester Junc. box	
Alton and Tisted	Alton box	Electric train tablet system (Tyer's No 6)
Alton signal box	Butts Junc.	
	Faringdon Halt	
	Tisted box	
Tisted & West Meon	Tisted box	Electric train tablet system (Tyer's No 6)
Tisted signalbox	Between 56 and 56¼ m.p.	
	Privett	
	Near 59¾ m.p.	
	West Meon box	
West Meon & Droxford	West Meon box	Electric train tablet system (Tyer's No 6)
West Meon box	Between 63¾ and 64 m.p.	
	Droxford box	
Droxford & Wickham	Droxford box	Electric train tablet system (Tyer's No 6)
Droxford box	Between 67¼ and 67½ m.p.	
	Mislingford Siding	
	Wickham box	*(There is no mention of the system continuing to the southern end of the MV line from Wickham to Knowle Junc.)*
Ashwater & Launceston	Ashwater box	Electric train tablet system (Tyer's No 3)
Launceston signalbox	Tower Hill	
	Launceston box	
Harpledown Junc. & Lyminge	Harpledown Junc.	Electric train token system
Harpledown Junc.	Canterbury South	
	Bridge	
	Bishopsbourne	
	Berham	
	Wigmore Siding	
	Eltham	
	Ottings Siding	
	Lyminge	

(No mention is made of the installations on Hawkhurst, Lydd, New Romney, Dungeness and Appledore systems.)

(Readers with an interest in trolley working may care to peruse the book *Great Western Aspects*, where a detailed article on the Great Western occupation key system will be found.)

SOUTHERN RAILWAY.

INSTRUCTION No. 10a. (1932.)

Instructions as to the occupation of the single line between Ashwater and Launceston by the Engineer's Department.

1. In connection with the occupation of the single line between Ashwater and Tower Hill or between Tower Hill and Launceston by a trolley, or for the carrying out of repairs or other operations which would render the running of trains unsafe, a method of control by means of occupation-keys has been brought into use, and, provided the man in charge of the trolley or the Ganger, as the case may be, is in possession of the relative occupation-key for the section of line to be occupied, it will not be necessary for Flagmen to be sent out for protective purposes.

2. Occupation-key boxes and telephones are provided as shown below:—

Station	Position of occupation-Key box and telephone
Ashwater	In signal box.
Tower Hill	On platform, near Booking Office.
Launceston	In signal box.

A control instrument is also provided in the signal box at Launceston and the method of obtaining and replacing the occupation-keys is as set out in the undermentioned instructions.

3. To obtain the occupation-key at Ashwater, Tower Hill or Launceston the switch of the control instrument at Launceston must first be turned from No. 1 (normal) to No. 2 position and the occupation-key at Ashwater, Tower Hill or Launceston, according to the place at which such key is required to be withdrawn, must be turned so that the index on the relative occupation-key box shows No. 2 position. The Signalmen at Ashwater and Launceston must then hold down the bell key of their respective tablet instruments for five seconds during which time the switch of the control instrument at Launceston must be turned to No. 4 position. This will cause the word "free" to appear on the indicator of the occupation-key box in which the occupation-key has been turned to No. 2 position and this key must thereupon be turned so that the index shows No. 3 position. The occupation-key can then be withdrawn.

Occupation-keys may, if necessary, be released for the occupation of the Ashwater–Tower Hill and Tower Hill–Launceston sections simultaneously.

4. To restore the occupation-key at Ashwater, Tower Hill or Launceston it must be placed in the relative occupation-key box and the key turned to the right until the index shows No. 1 position. In cases where an occupation-key has been replaced in the relative occupation-key box at Ashwater or Tower Hill, the Signalman at Ashwater, or Engineer's Department man at Tower Hill, as the case may be, must so advise the Signalman at Launceston by telephone.

Meanwhile, back on the Southern, Waterloo was already coming up with its own ideas for expansion and was considering the following routes:

Ashford	to	Canterbury West
Canterbury West	to	Minster
Ashford	to	Ore
Paddock Wood	to	Maidstone West
Hurst Green Junction	to	Ashurst Junction
Redgate Mill Junction	to	Culver Junction
Andover Junction #	to	Kimbridge Junction
Lymington Junction #	to	Broadstone Junction
Newton St Cyres	to	St Budeaux
Colyford	to	Copplestone
Umberleigh	to	Ilfracombe

Subsequent (1933) correspondence appears to indicate trolley working was not introduced on the lines marked # thus.

A point to mention is that power trolleys could well have worked on various lines under standard block regulations without the need for intermediate key boxes. Consequently, occupation key working was not applicable.

Left: The front page of the working instructions as applied between Ashwater and Launceston. These followed a standard format, as per the Mid Hants/Meon valley sheets seen earlier, and only differed so far as names and specific local instructions applied.

Below: An interesting sketch depicting the means of securing trolley and trailer. Whenever such pieces are located it always begs the question, 'why?' Presumably something had occurred to render such a drawing necessary.

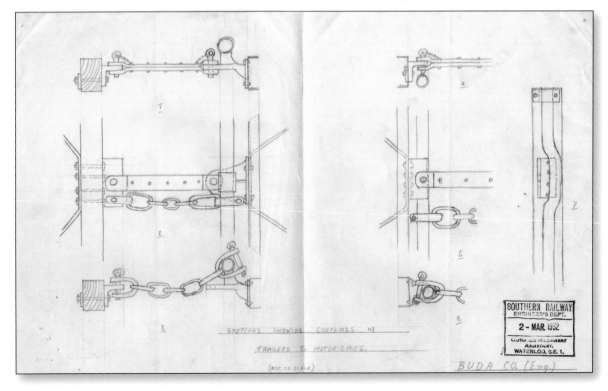

While a motor trolley was in itself progress so far as getting men to a work site quickly, there was a natural limit to how much material might be transported without adding a trailer. Consequently, the issue of adding a trailer was raised very early on. The consensus arrived at was that the trailer should have its own independent braking system and that a member of the gang should travel on the trailer able to operate the brakes if necessary. Again, the experience of the GWR was mainly sought when compiling working instructions involving trolleys and trailers, some of which stated what was perhaps obvious:

'Care must be taken to ensure all materials carried are within gauge. No man must be allowed to sit on the front of the trailer or on the back of the trolley with a trailer in tow.' (The LMS did not necessarily use intermediate key boxes and instead provided a bicycle that was carried on the trailer. Instead, a member of the gang would ride the bicycle to and from the relevant signal box to return or collect the 'token', allowing the trolley to be restored to the track. A reply from the LNER referred to that company using motor trolleys that are required to exhibit a white light to the front and a red light to the rear. On the LNER, trolley operation was also only permitted on a specified list of lines.)

Hand trolley at Eastleigh 1962. *A. E. West*

Where to park your trolley and keep it out of the way! This is the loading platform of the Outdoor Machinery Department at Eastleigh, which had a siding alongside the up main line just south of Eastleigh station.

Appendix 1

Taken from the Wickham Works List, trolleys ordered by the
Southern Railway to 31/12/1947.

Date	Car No	Type	Running No	Destination
23-7-31	408	17 Long Framed		Paddock Wood
30-9-31	436	17		Ashford
30-9-31	437	17		Exmouth
30-9-31	438	17		Ashford
30-9-31	439	17		Ashford
30-10-31	455	17		Ashford
18-1-33	919	17		Exeter
18-1-33	920	17		Exeter
18-1-33	921	17		Exeter
18-1-33	922	17		Exeter
18-1-33	923	17		Exeter
30-1-33	925	17	22	Exeter
30-1-33	926	17	23	Exeter
30-1-33	927	17	24	Exeter
30-1-33	928	17	25	Exeter
30-1-33	929	17	26	Alton
30-1-33	930	17	27	Alton
30-1-33	931	17	28	Alton
30-1-33	932	17	29	Alton
30-1-33	933	17	30	Alton
30-1-33	934	17	31	Ashford
30-1-33	935	17	1	Exeter
30-1-33	936	17	2	Exeter
30-1-33	937	17	3	Alton
30-1-33	938	17	4	Alton
7-2-33	939	17	5	Alton
7-2-33	940	17	6	Alton
7-2-33	941	17	7	Alton
7-2-33	942	17	8	Ashford
7-2-33	943	17	32	Exeter
7-2-33	944	17	33	Exeter
7-2-33	945	17	34	Exeter
14-2-33	946	17	35	Exeter
7-2-33	947	17	36	Exeter
7-2-33	948	17	37	Exeter
?	949	17	38	Exeter
14-2-33	950	17	39	Exeter
14-2-33	951	17	40	Exeter
14-2-33	952	17	41	Exeter
21-2-33	953	17	42	Templecombe S & D section

Date	Car No	Type	Running No	Destination
21-2-33	954	17	51	Templecombe S & D section
21-2-33	955	17	52	Templecombe S & D section
21-2-33	956	17	53	Templecombe S & D section
21-2-33	957	17	54	Templecombe S & D section
21-2-33	958	17	55	Templecombe S & D section
21-2-33	959	17	56	Templecombe S & D section
21-2-33	960	17	57	Templecombe S & D section
21-2-33	961	17	58	Templecombe S & D section
21-2-33	962	17	59	Templecombe S & D section
17-5-33	1118	17	43	Ashford
17-5-33	1119	17	44	Ashford
17-5-33	1122	17T	Trailer No 9	Ashford
27-6-34	1555	17	46	Ashford
31-8-34	1644	17	47	Exmouth Junction
31-1-36	2020	17T		Horsmonden
14-9-36	2134	17T		Queensferry
24-10-40	2962	17A	48	

Aside from the books referenced in the text, the author would also like to thank Mike King and also refer readers to:

The Wickham Works List by Keith Gunner and Michael Kennard, published by Denis Duck Publications 2004.

Wickham of Ware by Loxley G. Ford and James Cooper Jn., published by The Rockingham Press 2003.

Service Stock of the Southern Railway by R. W. Kidner (revised by David Gould), published by the Oakwood Press 1998.

The Lost Archives of Stephen Townroe
Part 2

In issue No 36 (October) we were delighted to include the first selection of images from the unseen archive of the late Stephen Townroe.

For this issue we have made a further trawl (and with many more still to come). 'SCT' was adept at not only recording his own experiences, but also when he witnessed something which to him was unusual. The only regret we might have is the ability to ask, 'Why were you at?' As ever, I am grateful for the assistance given by the Townroe family in the compilation of these pages.

The sight of a workforce in their thousands entering or leaving the works at the start and end of the shift was once common at any one of the many steam workshops (and no doubt other engineering facilities) for decades. It was a view we all saw, yet how many recorded it? Here it is happening at Eastleigh in June 1937, the men having used No 1 gate, which was accessed by a flight of steps directly off the end of Campbell Road bridge. In the background a selection of engines may be seen, always facing into the works – a feature that continued throughout steam days.

On the up main at Farnborough. Perhaps slightly unusually SCT was in the train this time rather than on the loco. This was one of several taken on the same occasion between Basingstoke and Surbiton – either the speed was less for this one or he had managed to master camera shake as the others were unfortunately blurred. No doubt the reason for the view was to record one of the signal gantries with its respective co-acting arms: a train obviously expected on the down main. Notice the 'Down slow to down yard' home signal is of conventional mechanical type with no repeating arm further down the post. The circular storage tank at this end of the signal box was the air reservoir for the pneumatic signals either side of the station. Taken early autumn 1937.

Later in the same year we have a short series of views entitled 'spray cleaning of engines at Stewarts Lane'. This was in the same batch, although rather than cleaning this clearly shows former SECR B1 4-4-0 No 1448 being readied for its next turn of duty.

The spray cleaning mentioned. This would appear to have been as much steam as spray cleaning and was an experiment that was being conducted by several railways around this time. No doubt it was intended to reduce the demands on manpower as well as remove grime from otherwise inaccessible areas. Neither was there a purely aesthetic reason behind this for dirt and grime could mask a defect: a missing, damaged or broken component, which might otherwise cause danger. The engine being dealt with is C class 0-6-0 No (3)1719, the one disadvantage of the exercise being the amount of water and mess created. For whatever reason, this type of cleaning does not appear to have been used above the footplate nor was it perpetuated after the Second World War.

A visit to Dover saw SCT record a number of images of the train ferry operating from there, together with the SS *Shepperton Ferry*. Built new for the Southern Railway by Swan Hunter in 1934, the vessel was 346ft 8in in length and powered by four turbines, giving a service speed of up to 16 knots. Her original capacity was twelve sleeping cars (the Night Ferry service), or forty wagons. In addition she could take 25 cars and 500 passengers. Requisitioned by the Admiralty in 1939 she was converted to a mine layer appropriately with the name HMS *Shepperton*. At the same time she was armed with a 4in anti-aircraft gun and two .303 machine guns. She could carry 270 mines. Subsequent war service saw her in the role of troopship and a heavy lift vessel, for which she was equipped with a crane to lift steam locos. She was returned to the Southern Railway post-Second World War and continued to serve, mainly, on the Dover to Dunkirk route until being withdrawn and scrapped in 1972.

The water softener at Horsham steam depot – and in the foreground part of the new electrical installation for the expansion of the third-rail in 1937. We may wonder why this view was taken – we can be certain it had little to do with the brassicas in the foreground! Whatever, it is actually quite prophetic as some years later, when he had just taken charge at Eastleigh, an engine that had been transferred there from Horsham suffered the collapse of the firebox crown, the cause of which was the condition of the water supply at Horsham. Just visible is one of the members of the ubiquitous C2X class, long associated with Horsham steam shed, and beyond this a glimpse of part of the depot breakdown train.

While in the area of Horsham, SCT took the time to record the movement of a Stroudley D1 0-4-2T and single horsebox. We may assume this was being shunted within station limits – perhaps having been detached or due to be attached to a main line service. This was known both officially and literally as 'tail' traffic – so called as such a vehicle would be at the very end of the train.

It was, and indeed still is, for rolling stock to be cascaded on to lesser duties as newer and more modern replacement become available. Here is an example at Guildford prior to the Second World War with what may well be its 'more modern' replacement alongside. (The actual vehicle is a former LCDR 27ft six-wheeled passenger brake van, built in July 1880 at Longhedge: LCDR No 67. It became SECR No 528 after 1899 and then SR van No 417 in 1923, then to SR Diagram 878 – one of about thirty to become SR property. In September 1935 the van was transferred to departmental stock as No 920s and allocated to the loco running department at Guildford, being seen on this duty in the picture. It was withdrawn on 8 May 1940. Quite a number of them were used as departmentals from the mid-1920s onwards. The van to the right, 949s: is an ex-LSWR 30ft passenger brake allocated similarly. *With grateful thanks to Mike King*

Below and opposite: One of the pair of Neilson crane-tank engines delivered new to the SECR in 1881 and seen here at an unknown location, possibly Lancing. As will be seen, only rudimentary protection was provided for the crew, hence their rigging of 'storm sheets' front and originally rear. In late 1938 this engine was sent for overhaul and emerged with an enclosed cab after, which it was based at Stewarts Lane and assisted in shunting of the CWS milk depot nearby. It remained in use until July 1949.

Above: 'And getting paid for doing it'! One of the tasks given to SCT was to ride on the footplate of Lord Nelson No 857 after it had been fitted with an experimental taper boiler. However, we are not told where these observations took place nor his conclusions.

Left: Finally for this issue, a photograph of King Arthur No 769 *Sir Balan* leaving the unmistakable vista of Dover Marine.

As we were preparing this issue for submission and checking, a letter arrived from Keith Dawe, who identified himself as a former Eastleigh man. Keith provides an interesting snippet on one of our earlier articles, 'The Salisbury Goods', which appeared in SW35 – see this issue's Rebuilt – and it was while in discussion with Keith on his time at Eastleigh that the subject of Mr Townroe came up. The rest is best stated in Keith's own words, 'Yes I know, or knew most of the Eastleigh men mentioned at various times in your excellent publication. Alas, as it is now nigh on half a century ago since we lost our steam engines, most of the old steam drivers are now gone and even those of us who were just nippers trying to do a grown man's job – I was seventeen when I was booked my first up and down (i.e. Waterloo and back) turn – have now enjoyed several years of retirement.

'We do meet up from time to time at the enginemen's reunion. Some I would have fired too on occasion, others I knew by name only. Hugh (Abbinett), of course, I know of, Cyril Stephens I think was a running toreman at Eastleigh Shed, unless I am mistaken.

'Stephen Townroe – who I always thought was a Sid Townroe – was one down from God. He was the chief loco inspector and there was absolutely no way that a young insignificant fireman would call him by his Christian name, no matter what he thought it was!

'I did have dealings with Mr Townroe and have happy memories of the occasion.

'I do not now remember the exact date, but again I was only 17 or 18 and we were booked up and down 10.30. I did not have my regular driver, so I would have been in the Holiday Relief Link at the time and having worked up to Waterloo part way on an up freight to Basingstoke, thence a commuter train – all stations to Surbiton then fast to Waterloo – we had our break upon relief at Waterloo and in turn relieved Nine Elms men, who brought our engine on to the stock for the down 10.30

'As we walked down the platform on the Monday morning, my driver remarked that it looked as though he was going to have an easy ride home, but it was tough luck on me.

'Mr Townroe was stood by the engine with a fireman who was about to undergo the dreaded driving exam under the observation of the great man himself, prior to hopefully passing out for driving.

'The same happened each day of that week and I have to say that it was a bit of an experience working under the watchful gaze of S. C. T. and trying to fire to someone who was as nervous as a kitten and in such a state of anxiety that they didn't even realise they had a fireman, let alone acknowledge his presence. Fortunately I knew the road well enough and I also knew which signals were mine to relay to the driver. I soon found that it was Mr Townroe who was looking over to me and acknowledging my relaying of signal information with a smile and a thumbs up.

'On the final day we ran into Eastleigh, where we were to be relieved and I had prepared the footplate in the usual manner by hosing it down, etc; had a wash in a bucket of water and was all set to be off for the walk down to the loco and sign off while Mr Townroe took his man to one side for a debriefing.

'Then to my horror Mr Townroe put his hand out to stop me getting off the engine. "Just a minute young man," he said. And, of course, horror struck the very heart of me – what had I done?

'With a smile he said, "Thank you fireman, you did very well especially for such a young man – but there is just one thing I must say." and pointing to my neck he said, "I don't like a man who doesn't wash behind his ears."

'Bearing in mind that I was, and still am very blonde, every speck of black coal dust used to stick to me like glue and its presence was very obvious in contrast to my natural colour.'

Fifty Years on
The End of Steam Working on the Isle of Wight

In recalling the events of half a century back on the Isle of Wight, the years 1966–67 were a low point for the railway.

Already in the 1950s the Bembridge, Freshwater, Ventnor West, and Newport to Sandown lines had ceased operation, while starting in February 1966 the route between Cowes and Newport and on to Smallbrook Junction closed permanently, although goods would continue to be handled until May as the track was destined to remain in situ for over a year. Then, in April 1966, Shanklin to Ventnor ceased operation, leaving a single route only from Ryde Pier Head as far as Shanklin.

'The railway, as was: 1.' A typical scene at Ryde St Johns Road recorded in the summer of 1965. A solitary passenger awaits a southbound train while behind, No 27 *Merstone* awaits the return of its crank axle. *P. Hocquard*

'The railway, as was: 2.' "Is it this way or the other?" The crew of No W24 *Calbourne*, also at Ryde St Johns, in September 1966. *Rod Hoyle*

Under the original Beeching plan all the island lines would have closed, save for a short section from Ryde Pier Head to St Johns – how this would have been practical is hard to justify. In the event, closure was restricted to the routes above and the decision taken to electrify the remaining line to the now southernmost terminus at Shanklin. But electrification work on an existing route was not easy and thus the decision was made to suspend public services at the end of 1966 to allow engineers full access. Under what was then deemed 'total possession', the engineers could now work freely on the 8¼-mile section using (ironically) motive power in the form of two members of the 'O2' class, W24 *Calbourne* and W31 *Chale*, especially retained for works trains.

Attempts at revitalising the network with a private enterprise railcar operation in 1967 came to nothing, although fortunately No W24, together some representative examples of carriage and goods rolling stock, were saved and now form the nucleus of the collection for the Isle of Wight steam railway. All other stock was scrapped.

Services recommenced now using former London Transport tube stock modified to operate on a third rail electric system, instead using separate collection and return conductor rails. The new service commenced in March 1967 and continues to this day, although the original tube stock has since been replaced, this time with a different batch of redundant LT stock, while rationalisation of resources have seen sidings (just two remain at Ryde St Johns and Sandown) and loops removed and signalling similarly contracted. Even so, two new stations have opened, Smallbrook Junction, where an interchange is made with the Isle of Wight steam railway, and at Lake, between Sandown and Shanklin.

The Isle of Wight steam railway has its headquarters at Haven Street and runs east–west from Smallbrook Junction to Wootton – and is well worth a visit.

Above: 'The railway, as was: 3.' Perhaps pondering his own, if not the railway's future. A lone member of staff and stock typifying the 'old' railway, Ryde, December 1966. *Rod Hoyle*

Left: 'Transition 1'. For a period in late 1966, trains between Ryde Esplanade and Ryde St Johns Road were 'top and tailed' due to engineering work at the Pierhead, which meant run-round facilities were no longer available at the terminus. Here one such working is seen, W16 (with W28 at the rear) on the 0930 Ryde to Shanklin approaching St Johns, on 11 December 1966. *M. Dunnett*

'Transition 2'. Meanwhile, back on the mainland, redundant London transport tube stock had been selected for use and was being marshalled at Micheldever ready for transfer to the Island. Much (if not all) the electrical modifications were undertaken at Wimbledon, after which it was not uncommon to see a former tube train scooping along the main line west of Wimbledon on test. *John Bailey*

'Transition 3'. The former LT stock was transferred to the Island and towed by steam engine to the works at Ryde St Johns. Of necessity, a barrier wagon with modified couplings was required, seen here in the shape of a converted box van now numbered DS46951 attached to a former control trailer now numbered S38S. The safety chain may be noted. *Dr J. Mackett*

'Transition 5'. 'New' trains awaiting service at St Johns. The depot here would be retained for servicing the electric units and still retain their safety chains. Note also the clean insulator pots supporting the newly laid conductor rail.

'Transition 6' and in service. An electric unit has its red disc attached at what was now the end of the line at Shanklin, ready for the return to Ryde. The driver is still in 'steam'-type garb, while between the sleepers, evidence of former steam trains still remain.

Opposite: 'Transition 4'. Although on paper all might have appeared satisfactory, practical clearance checks were also made: as here with gauging taking place at Shanklin on 4 September 1966. *Dr J. Mackett*

Above: Meanwhile, with the few exceptions already mentioned, the now redundant steam engines and associated rolling stock was worked to Newport, where it was destined to be stabled until the time came for scrap. This was the scene at Newport on Easter Monday, 27 March 1967, No 27 leading a line-up of redundant engines and stock that extended into all three platforms. *G. S. Cocks*

Left: Actual dismantling of the engines was undertaken by a local company on what had once been part of the former Freshwater line. Here the brass surround from a cab spectacle has been removed and will be stored separately.

Opposite: Seen from the station footbridge, the whole presented a melancholy sight; the engines, station and former route to Cowes disappear into the distance. A scrap merchant's delight but a rail enthusiast's nightmare. *Alastair McIntyre*

And so as time slipped away, the once proud fleet of steam engines was slowly confined to history – exactly as would the coal yard in the foreground.

Ironically perhaps, while the engines and stock had been delivered to Newport ready for scrapping, once arrived, there was no easy method of moving them to their required position for dismantling. Consequently it was found necessary to steam one of the O2s for the purpose!

Of the two O2s retained for engineering work, W24, was saved for preservation but W31 was not so lucky. It is seen here in Ryde coal yard in the process of being cut up, recorded from the cab of a passing electric unit on 29 August 1967.
Graham S. Cocks

Many of the O2s on the Island had a life in excess of thirty years, although not the first generation of electric sets that had been transferred in 1967, such as No S93 from former 3TIS set No 486 033, awaiting scrap at Ryde on 13 June 1982.
Brian Morrison

Meanwhile, a few miles south, the former Ventnor Town station slumbered. No longer will day trippers and holidaymakers alike throng its platforms, just one of numerous casualties of the move from rail to road. Despite various recommendations and attempts at extending the railway back from Shanklin to the former terminus here, as time passes this would seem ever less likely. The site is now transformed from railway to an industrial estate.

But What If ...

In preparing these notes for this commemorative feature, I have had the privilege of corresponding with Mark Brinton, former BR engineer and definite IOW railway aficionado. Mark has kindly provided detail of the 'what if' timeline, which details the proposal to transfer 'modern' steam locomotives to the island to replace the O2s.

While many readers will have believed this was a 'late in the day' mid-1960s alternative to electrification, its origins can actually be traced back to the previous decade (just) when it was recorded that No 84027 had arrived at Eastleigh in the period ending 12 December 1959. At the time, the reason for the move was not specified. However, a few weeks earlier on 12 November 1959, the Eastleigh Drawing Office Register shows a first drawing prepared indicating the class of locomotive as 'prepared' for use on the Island. The main work involved cutting down the cab and redesigning the chimney, both necessary to comply with the restricted IOW loading gauge. Mark also quotes from an internal document of the time, 'The reason for the (proposed) conversion was because the cost of casting new cylinders for the O2s was excessive.

They (the O2s' cylinder walls) were getting very thin (due to reboring over the years) and many would require replacement in the near future.'

Meanwhile, in December 1959 it was reported that Nos 84020–3 and 84024–9 had been allocated to 73F (Ashford) and 73G (Ramsgate) respectively.

How long No 84027 of the Ramsgate batch remained at Eastleigh is not certain but it may well have been present simply to be able to check drawing details against an actual member of the class. The first batch of actual drawings covering the chimney, boiler, cab, injectors and motion plate was prepared on 21 January 1960. (It is not clear if this is the date the aforesaid drawings were completed or perhaps even reference numbers allocated for work due to start, or in progress.)

According to the *Railway Observer,* Nos 84020, 21, 25 and 29 from the Ashford/Ramsgate allocations were noted as arrived at Eastleigh Works for the period ending 30 January, certainly giving the impression at least that the concept was to go ahead.

BR Class 2 tank No 84028 recorded at Ashford on 19 March 1961.
Rod Blencowe

The February issue of the *RO* also gave details of the proposed BR condemnation programme for Southern Region steam locomotives during 1960, twelve members of the O2 class to be withdrawn, leaving nineteen in stock. In the event there was a change of heart as, according to Bradley, just two members of the class – both mainland examples – succumbed in 1960, meaning twenty-two of the twenty-six IOW examples were, on paper at least, still regarded as operationally available.

Meanwhile, in March 1960 the potential for the use of 'modern' steam engines on the Southern as a replacement for older types was being developed further with a belief that either the BR 84xxx type or the Ivatt Class 2 equivalent should be tested on the Axminster to Lyme Regis route. (One other branch where elderly locomotives were totally dominant was from Havant to Hayling Island, although here it would have been weight rather than loading gauge restrictions that would have precluded a larger steam type and no mention has been found to suggest this was ever considered.)

In the same month we arrive at what is summarised in the RCTS book *A Detailed History of BR Standard Steam Locomotives Volume 3*, where there is mention that at the same time there was a proposal to modify three engines of the 84xxx type for use on the Island. No doubt in connection with this, No 84020 arrived at Eastleigh Works 'period ending' 7 May 1960, while in April the *RO* reported further progress that the conversion work on the three should be complete by the end of May. While some of the necessary gauging work may appear to have been reasonably simple, such as shortening the chimney by 3in and removing the cab-side windscreens, the reported necessary reduction in width of 7in over the cylinders was far from straightforward.

Meanwhile, Eastleigh was continuing with further drawings. In April there was a second batch covering necessary brake system modifications (Westinghouse brake equipment perhaps?). In the following month what was stated as the last drawing was produced, covering the reservoir support brackets (which does tend to imply the Westinghouse air brake was to be fitted, although this is still not confirmed 100 per cent as the engines would still have a vacuum brake reservoir as well, of course).

Information reported as coming from *Railway Observer* originated from observers 'on the ground'. Some were visitors to the works (and various sheds) at a time when it was possible to arrange society visits on a regular basis. Information might also be obtained from conversations with those on the inside and 'in the know', while several *RO* members and contributors were also railway (including 'works') employees.

It was also not just the *RO* that had its sources. In May 1960 *Trains Illustrated*, the forerunner of *Modern Railways*, picked up the same theme, that No 84020 was to be modified for IOW use upon its next overhaul. In the event it was sister engine No 84022 that arrived at Eastleigh soon afterwards; according to the *RO* this took place in the period ending 9 July 1960.

Meanwhile, elsewhere on BR other departments were in the process of considering the very future of what remained of the island railway network, already curtailed by now to the Ryde–Ventnor, and Ryde–Newport–Cowes routes. The investigation centred on the most economic method of working the lines and, according to a contemporary piece in the *Isle of Wight County Press*, included the option of using diesel traction either in the form of locomotives or multiple units.

Even so, it appeared that progress with a 2-6-2T was going ahead as again it was the *RO* that reported that in August 1960 the necessary work was:

1 New chimney 6½in shorter.
2 Dome casing reduced by $2^{1/16}$ in
3 Cab roof lowered by 1in
4 Cab side windscreens removed
5 Substitute of vacuum brake equipment for compressed air to be used for train braking. Engine steam brake to be retained.

The report continued that initially only a single locomotive was to be modified – presumably No 84022. It was also noted that the modifications were different to those that had been reported earlier, especially as there is no mention of reducing the width over the cylinders.

As if to confirm matters, No 84022 was noted by several observers at the August 1960 Eastleigh open day, although at the time still in its 'as built' form.

Shortly afterwards a trial with Ivatt class 2 No 41297 took place on the Lyme Regis branch. The presence/existence of the 84xxx series of engines on the Southern Region generally now forms several entries in Mark's text complemented by the records of another *RO* correspondent, who in February 1961 visited the island to detail the whereabouts and operational position of the O2s.

So far as the 84xxx engines were concerned the references were as follows:

December 1960	Nos 84020–9 now allocated to 73F
10 February 1961	Nos 84020 transferred to 73A
13 March 1961	No 84029 reported as having arrived at Eastleigh Works prior to 11 April 61

10 April 1961	Allocation of 84xxx series engines on the SR as follows:
	    Nos 84020–3 at 72A
	    Nos 84024–7 at 75A
	    Nos 84028–9 at 71A
	    (No 84020 arrived on Eastleigh Works by 13 May 61

May 1961	Nos 84020–3 now allocated to 72A
10 June 1961	No 84028 reported as having arrived at Eastleigh Works prior to 8 July 61
September 1961	Nos 84020–9 transferred to the LMR in exchange for Nos 41320/4/7–9, and Nos 41325–6 from the NER.
10 October 1961	All SR allocated 84xxx have now been transferred to the LMR.

Former mainland (Plymouth Friary based) O2 No 30183 withdrawn at the end of September 1961 and seen on the scrap line at Eastleigh the following month. It was dismantled at the nearby works in November 1961 and may have been one of the class to yield parts to assist in keeping the IOW engines operational. *J. Eyers*

So where did this leave the position so far as a 'modern' steam replacement for the O2s was concerned? Well, to answer this we have to go back slightly to the *RO* for March 1961 where a correspondent (unnamed) reported that, 'One or two boilers from withdrawn "mainland" O2s have been transferred to the Island, also that no Standard 2-6-2Ts are now expected on the Island.'

A bland but, as it turned out, accurate statement, although it does not in any way answer the question as to why the idea was shelved. Bear in mind this was two years prior to Beeching (whose report would recommend closure of all the island lines). We may therefore only speculate on several points without any confirmation that any are correct – perhaps a separate report existed concerning possible closure of the island system; or was it cost of the conversations allied to possible additional necessary modifications to infrastructure on the island; finally the possibility of a longer term replacement using diesel traction, etc? One other point not mentioned was the lifespan of the existing passenger rolling stock. The proposed modifications to the 84xxx type we now know would have involved the fitting of a Westinghouse pump for the air-braked carriage stock but nowhere is there mention of a modern replacement for what was already a collection of antiquated passenger vehicles.

Recent research suggests that BR expected to have closed all the island lines by the end of 1965. The CM&EE is quoted in reports that the coaching stock would last at least until then but that the O2 locos would not go beyond that date without a return to the mainland for extensive overhauls. There is very little in the Kew files on IOW policy referencing the replacement steam locomotives. This suggests that it was a CM&EE routine decision resulting from the condemnation programme and the need to maintain services until instructed otherwise. Presumably if the costs of the scheme had exceeded the CM&EE's financial authority then he would have sought additional authority from the general manager. Paperwork would then have been generated that would

subsequently have found its way into the Kew archives. It is likely (although yet to be confirmed) that the project was cancelled because the withdrawal of the mainland O2s was considered adequate to generate enough spares for the continued operation of enough locomotives to meet island requirements until the end of 1965 without the need to fund the modification and transportation of the three Class 2 tank engines.

For the next four years the trail goes cold, but then on 25 May 1965 the Eastleigh Drawing Office Register records a new drawing having been produced for a chimney for a Class 2 tank engine. It was not specified if this was for the 84xxx or Ivatt type. The next month saw a second drawing prepared, this time for the left-hand side tank.

These drawings pre-empted what was reported in *Wight Report No 101* 'An Island Might Have Been' by Mike Kennard, in which he states that in late 1965 plans for the use of 84xxx type engines were revived for the simple reason that most of the island O2s were simply beyond economical repair. Former Eastleigh works inspector Mark Abbott recalls that on his periodic visits to Ryde as a steam loco inspector he was never popular, simply because he would invariably condemn another O2 as unfit for service. However, he did redeem himself on another occasion when, outside the back of Eastleigh Works, he came across a new but un-machined cylinder casting for an O2, which was promptly seized upon and subsequently used.

Behind the scenes we may now imagine the next stage with a request sent to the LMR for an 84xxx series engine to be transferred to the Southern 'at the earliest opportunity'. Already though a number of members of the class had been withdrawn from the LMR and lay around awaiting a decision on their fate. It should be added that engines were withdrawn usually for one of two reasons; either the services they had previously worked no longer existed and there was no further work for them or, and this was more usual, defect/condition issues had occurred that, with the accelerating decline of steam generally, meant that repairs were either not able to be authorised or were not deemed to be cost-effective considering the limited life remaining for steam generally. A third reason could also be when a diktat arrived from above to the effect that all remaining members of a particular type were to be withdrawn – as per the K class (and others) on the SR at the end of 1962.

In the event No 84014 was the selected engine and on 24 October 1965 was observed being towed south through Bramley (between Reading and Basingstoke) by No 76033. It was not destined to be a happy journey for just a few miles on at Basingstoke No 84014 developed a hot box and was shunted to the running shed there for attention.

Repairs were undertaken quickly because the very next day the engine was recorded at Basingstoke, this time in steam and in charge of a Reading to Eastleigh van train. Evidently No 84014 completed this turn, indeed your editor recalls seeing it 'cold' inside Eastleigh shed towards the end of 1965 among a line of out of use engines and being told at the time that it was destined for the Isle of Wight.

On paper at least ten further members of the 84xxx type were similarly transferred from the LMR to the SR in early November 1965, Nos 84010, 5, 8 and 28 booked to be hauled (dead) from the LMR at Lostock Hall to Fratton on 10 November.

However, the move never occurred and, again quoting Mike Kennard, 'Having had the opportunity to inspect No 84014, the SR authorities found it not to be in the best of health while moreover it was becoming clear that the other nine engines were in a similar state. This indicated that a lot of money would need to be spent on major overhauls additional to the cost of modifying and shipping the locomotives.'

In many ways this was hardly surprising, not least for the reasons mentioned earlier, bearing in mind as well the general condition of steam motive power was deteriorating all the time. The request to a shed foreman to transfer engines elsewhere, especially off-region, was a godsend in losing some lame ducks, the LMR by this time having the proverbial flock of them! Why the engines were to have been despatched to Fratton was explained later in the *RO* with the comment that the necessary modifications were to have been carried out at Ryde. (The shipping and movement arrangements would have been interesting, to Medina Wharf perhaps and possibly with various fittings, chimney, dome cover and cab removed?)

The reason for the decision to modify the locos at Ryde would appear to have been cost and the fact that Eastleigh Loco Works had already started the process of being converted into a locomotive and carriage works. At Eastleigh the iron foundry had already closed, which was why it was not possible

to cast replacement cylinders, hence the need to source these from withdrawn locos. So as far as the proposed conversions were concerned, it would appear that the parts to modify the locos would have been supplied by Eastleigh but with the work on the locos done at Ryde or possibly Newport had there been insufficient space at Ryde.

As to why the idea was resurrected again in 1964, there was a fear by the CM&EE that it could not maintain sufficient O2 locos (for the stated reasons) until the end of 1965 and that it was possible there would need to be a steam service maintained beyond that date due to the lack of any decision on the future of the island's railways. No evidence has yet come to light as to how it was intended to ship the replacement locos to the island. On the basis that the intended destination of the locos from the LMR was Fratton, this would suggest road haulage via car ferry, as was later used for the diesel shunter. If it had been intended to use the floating crane then the destination would have been Eastleigh/Southampton rather than Fratton.

Meanwhile, two from the batch due for the Southern, Nos 84019 and 25, were at Bolton pending transfer and where one (unspecified) had already acquired a 70H (Ryde) shedcode together with the designation 'Ryde' painted on the buffer beam. Bolton was perhaps in ever more of a hurry to let them go!

Meanwhile, at Eastleigh No 84014 remained moribund. Its condition probably confirmed it was unsuitable for further work and it was officially withdrawn on 11 December 1965 and subsequently reported as scrapped at Cashmore's, Newport (South Wales, not on the island) in 1966. Travelling in convoy

The BR variant of the Class 2 tank, represented here by No 41327 recorded at Brighton. Originally widespread throughout the Southern Region, the engines slowly migrated west as steam was superseded. The class was found on branch and pilot duties, the latter right to the very end of steam working. *Mark Abbott*

with Q1s Nos 33020 and 33027, No 84014 left Eastleigh around 26 March and is believed to have arrived in South Wales two days later. Some dispute still occurs regarding movements of No 84014 in its final moths, and likewise regional 'ownership', but the above information is given in good faith.

While all this had been going on back at Waterloo, an urgent search was going on for a replacement for the O2s for, notwithstanding Dr Beeching's proposal to close all the island lines, the minister's eventual decision was that the section from Ryde to Shanklin would remain. As is known, the decision was eventually made to use former LT stock, although before electrification was confirmed there had been talk of installing diesel–electric engines within the LT units.

With the decision finally made for electrification of the remaining island line, former LT electric units began to appear in greater numbers at this stage, albeit for now still in the London area. In the event, just one new item of motive power was shipped to the island, not a steam locomotive but diesel shunter No D2554, which would be used for engineering purposes when required. It was shipped from Portsmouth on 7 October 1966. The final part of the story came on 12 September 1967, two months after steam had finished on the Southern Region, and four months after the electric trains had started running on the island. This was the when the drawing office register carried the entry, 'All drawings prepared for modifications to Class 2 Tanks for IOW scrapped.' It was unlikely there were any steam locomotives left that could have been converted anyway. Copies of a few of the conversion drawings have survived and are now in the care of the IOW Steam Railway.

(Mark provides source information for all his information, many of which are quoted above, and as such verifies his assertions. The whole forms part of an (as yet) unpublished work on the island railways and I'm sure I'm not alone in stating that I very much look forward to reading it when it is complete.)

What might have been. A Southern Region local but not on the Island. Instead it is a Tonbridge to Dover service pulling away from Sandling Junction in July 1958 behind Class 2 No 84023. *Derek Cross*

The EPB Story
Part 5 – Bulleid Stock
David Monk-Steele

(Previous articles in this series appeared in issues 20, 24, 25, and 26)

Having decided that ten-car trains were the future solution to increased capacity, it was apparent that suitable new rolling stock was required. The 4SUB units did not have a two-car equivalent and adding unpowered trailers was regarded as undesirable because from 1940 onwards it had been policy to rid the Southern of this operating inconvenience. There were, it is true, a small class of 2NOL units but these already had defined duties. They were five-a-side sets with a proportion of first class seating and so would not be readily available to strengthen the eight-car 4SUB formation, and because the seating capacity would be sub-standard. Given as well that, as wooden-bodied stock, they were regarded as less safe and obsolete, the best that use of the 2NOL might

offer was as a stopgap. In fact, during the 1950s some 2NOL sets were declassified to all third, including some with the motors isolated, and were used in ten-car formations but this was the exception rather than the rule. It was therefore deemed necessary to design and build some two-coach motor suburban sets. At about the same time the suburban fleet was in transition, and it is appropriate now to consider how that transition affected the shape of the Southern Region's answer to the problems of meeting peak demand.

4EPB unit No 5034 leading sister set No 5183 and 2EPB No 5712 at Bexley on the 16.56 Dartford to Cannon Street (via Loop line) service, 31 July 1973. Ten-car formations such as these were used at peak times. *Brian Morrison*

By 1950 the 4SUB construction programme was evolving. The formation had standardised on eight-bay saloons in the two motor coaches, and a ten-bay saloon and a ten- (sometimes nine-) compartment trailer, all on a SR 62ft underframe with 8ft wheelbase trailer bogies. The trailer bogies were similar in design to those provided under the steam stock and had their origins on the SE&CR. Motor bogies were generally of an 8ft 9 in wheelbase known as 'Central' type. These were massive plate frame structures of heavy riveted construction. Leaf spring primary suspension with coil secondary suspension was provided. The body style was distinctly Bulleid in shape, a continuous curved profile making maximum use of the available loading gauge, with full-fronted cab ends featuring two large windows either side of a route indicator panel. There were individual doors to each bay or compartment, and the door drop light was surmounted by a small fixed top light to help standing passengers see the station name boards.

From the middle of 1950, a start had been made to withdraw the wooden-bodied, five-a-side, pre-war former 3SUB stock to provide underframes for new units. Most of these had, by 1950, been augmented by the insertion of new six-a-side compartment trailers, some of mixed steel and timber construction and others of the new 'all steel' design. At the same time, these sets were being reformed using the better trailer cars to release some of these six-a-side augmentation trailers for insertion into the new all-steel 4SUB stock. The old sets were taken to Newhaven (and sometimes to Horley), where the wooden bodies were removed and burned. The underframes were then hauled to Lancing Works in a goods train to be dismantled, reconditioned and reassembled, before sending them to Eastleigh. At Eastleigh the new all-steel bodies were manufactured on a jig, welded from steel sheet and sections. The new body was attached to the underframe, fitted out and painted on a production line, and the complete sets were assembled in Eastleigh yard. The first batch incorporated a former 'augmentation' compartment trailer, suitably modified to work with the new sets, so the initial order was for three carriages, all of saloon configuration. The supply of second-hand underframes was inadequate to fulfil the building programme, therefore Lancing Works continued to manufacture new underframes for 4SUB carriages at the same time.

The underframes were fabricated from steel section mainly connected by rivets. The outer solebars were channels facing outwards, strengthened in traditional SR style by angle section trusses attached to the outer solebars. Headstocks were also of channel. A pair of inner solebars was also provided and there were transverse members intermediately. Timber footboards were provided along the entire length of each coach attached to brackets riveted to the solebars. Additional footboards were provided on all bogies.

At first the output of standard SR 4SUB units was continued as before, but in November 1951 the first of the new design of four-car units appeared. It was intended that all these new sets would be carried on second-hand underframes entirely rebuilt from the pre-war stock, most of which were less than twenty years old. Superficially they were similar to the sets already under construction, especially from a passenger perspective, but technically they performed much better, accelerating and braking much more quickly, a factor essential in getting more out of the restrictive layout between London Bridge, Charing Cross and Cannon Street.

The design incorporated a number of changes that would mean it was no longer compatible with the existing suburban fleet. The biggest difference was the braking system, which included electro-pneumatic (EP) operation. This method had proved successful by experiments with some express stock and with the double-decker sets, and therefore Westinghouse non-interlocked electro-pneumatic brakes with self-lapping controllers were provided. Twin pipe Westinghouse air brakes were still present throughout the train but the normal control of air to the brake cylinders on each coach used electrically operated valves. The EP brake offered much quicker application and release because the electrically operated valves worked instantaneously instead of relying solely on a change of pressure in the brake pipe to (activate the triple valves, which could take a few seconds to be effective.

The multiple unit control system was also different, the arrangement of multiple unit jumpers now being incompatible with other stock, having twenty-seven pins in a round plug/socket. A lot of attaching and detaching in service was carried out at a platform, either alongside a cleaning gantry in a depot or at a station, so to make life easier and safer for shunters, the air pipes and the twenty-seven-way jumper coupler were mounted just underneath the 'fireman's' side window and a twenty-seven-way receptacle and duplicate air pipes beneath the driver's side window.

Pin allocation in the jumper couplers was as follows:

1	Retaining	15	Run back
2	Series	16	Control negative
3	Parallel negative	17	Auxiliary control
4	Forward	18	Light set
5	Reverse	19	Light trip
6	Reset	20	Loudaphone call
7	Weak Field	21	Loudaphone speech
8	Compressor Synchronisation	22	Not allocated
9	Auxiliary Control	23	Not allocated
10	EP brake application	24	Not allocated
11	EP brake holding	25	Not allocated
12	EP brake negative	26	Auxiliary power on
13	Control supply (local)	27	Not allocated
14	Control supply (remote)		

Within the set, power and control cables were carried along the roof in exposed steel conduits. At the coach ends were junction boxes attached at roof level, and from these flexible

Between Cannon Street and Borough Market Junction – the latter sometimes referred to as 'location critical' for a delay or incident here could well have a knock-on effect almost throughout the whole of the South Eastern suburban network – unit 5045 heads away from London with the 16.26 to Dartford and Sidcup, 7 June 1976. The roof detail referred to in the text shows up clearly in this view. *Brian Morrison*

jumpers crossed between vehicles. A heating cable also crossed between each motor coach and its adjacent trailer car, being taken to roof level in a conduit attached to the vehicle end. Lighting was similarly supplied from a motor coach to an adjacent trailer. The coach lighting lamp holders were mounted on the outside of the roof connected by steel conduit to the roof end junction boxes. In each compartment and above each seating bay were two incandescent bulbs, each side fed by an independent circuit. Half the lamps were connected to the battery side of the reverse current contactor and would remain alight if the motor generator supply failed.

To make attaching and detaching easier and safer, a cut down Pullman gangway buffer/rubbing plate was provided at the outer ends of a four-car set with a drop-head Buckeye coupler. In normal service the side buffers were retracted and played no part in operation. Should the Buckeye coupler fail, however, or if the unit was required to attach to a vehicle not fitted with Buckeye couplers, the Buckeye head could be lowered to reveal a standard drawhook and the side buffers were extended. An 'emergency' screw coupling normally kept in the guard's van would then be used instead. To accommodate the new coupler the rebuilt frames were significantly improved and strengthened. Between the coaches inside the set the normal SR pattern of centre buffer and semi-permanent three link coupling was retained.

A motor generator fed from the line supply was provided to supply the 70 volt electrical systems, and maintain battery charging, for lighting. This was a new departure for suburban stock (although not for the express sets and the double-decker), and the characteristic of the dimming of the carriage lights as a 4SUB crossed a junction was absent from the new trains.

Driver comfort was also greatly improved. A proper desk with an adjustable chair was provided, the control equipment and indicators were now all arranged on the desk to be easily within the driver's field of vision and the brightness of lamps could be adjusted. The side door to the cab was abolished and entry was solely through the guard's van via a sliding door. This helped to reduced draughts. A sliding window was provided alongside the driver's shoulder to allow him to look back if necessary, and a duplicate was provided on the offside. The three-panel cab end was slightly modified with smaller windscreens, and a central illuminated roller blind route indicator was fitted as standard. Trico–Folberth windscreen wipers that parked clear of the driver's vision when not in use and sunshields for the nearside window and windscreen were also fitted. A few 4SUB units had been fitted with roller blind indicators but the bulk of that fleet still retained stencil indicators.

Traction equipment was similar to the earlier 4SUB sets, with two 245hp traction motors under each motor coach and on the lightweight axle hung EE507 type weighing 1.9 tons apiece. Current was collected by cast iron gravity shoes hung from a timber shoe beam attached to the axleboxes at either side of the motor bogies. The traction power was taken along a train line with jumpers between coaches within the set. This ensured that normally at least one collector shoe was in contact with the live rail at all times. Each shoe had a copper strip fuse in an arc chute mounted just above it, and there was a similar copper strip train line fuse suspended under the motor coach.

Originally the 4EPB sets were provided with power jumpers at the outer ends as well, but these fell into disuse and were being removed by 1954, although a shed trolley socket was retained to enable them to be moved under power in sheds where there was no third rail using a power cable attached to an overhead trolley wire. The first batch of the rebuilt sets numbered, 5001 to 5053, had 9ft wheelbase Eastern motor bogies, (formerly provided under 3SUB sets 1401 to 1534), when new, but the series starting at 5101 was fitted with the standard 8ft 9in version. The Eastern bogies could be distinguished by the guard irons, which were cranked, whereas the standard ones were straight, As spare 8ft 9in wheelbase became available at overhaul, those in the earlier series were brought into line with the rest of the fleet. Traction power was controlled from a master controller on the driver's desk, unlocked by a key. This in turn released a reversing and power handle. The master switch provided power to the control circuits and the electro-pneumatic brake circuits, which was controlled through a relay. This removed the need for a driver to carry a brake control key. The master controller had four positions, namely: shunting, full series, full parallel and parallel weak field. A current limit relay allowed the traction current to be used to provide maximum acceleration dependent upon which series or parallel position was selected.

The power control equipment was slung under the motor coaches, and consisted of lightweight electro-pneumatic unit switches, which incorporated cam-operated silver butt auxiliary contacts. The starting resistances were of expanded metal, saving up to two-thirds of the weight of the cast iron resistances previously fitted to SR electric stock.

As the control systems were fed from the 70 volt battery, a 'no-current' relay was incorporated to return the control equipment to the shunting position on loss of conductor rail supply, and to permit notching up to the state dictated by the master controller as soon as the supply was restored.

The parking brake was situated in the driving cab in front of the 'fireman's side' windscreen. It was a hand wheel mounted on a pillar, and was just visible from outside. A common practice at stabling points was to use a 'shoe paddle' propped against the wheel to indicate in which cab the handbrake was applied.

Under each seat in the passenger accommodation were totally enclosed electric heaters. Heating was fed from the line supply and each trailer was supplied from an adjacent motor coach. The heaters were thermostatically controlled and did not require intervention by the train crew.

The lighting in passenger accommodation was controlled from the guard's position by a 'trip and set' switch operated from any brake van. One pair of lamps in each guard's van was fed separately from the lighting circuit independent of the passenger accommodation. This was so the guard could see if there was a feed to his 'trip and set' lighting switch, and so there was also light available when the train was being operated empty and the passenger lighting was switched off.

On the South Western section, No 5105 is on the 14.12 Waterloo to Effingham Junction at Epsom, 25 March 1980. The distinctive signal box spanned the lines here from 1928 until 1990, when control was given over to Wimbledon panel. *Brian Morrison*

The other two lamps in the van were in the passenger lighting circuits and acted as 'pilot' lights.

The guard's vans, of which there was one in each motor coach, were each rated to carry 1 ton of parcels and mail, evenly distributed. Double doors were fitted on each side, one door being inward opening to allow the driver to enter or leave without fouling an adjacent line. The guard had an adjustable seat facing a desk against the inner wall, and on that wall was a periscope to enable him to observe signals and such like above the train roof. Also on that wall were the Westinghouse brake operating tap and gauges for train pipe and brake cylinder pressure, and a switch for the heater in the guard's van. A rack

for letter sorting and a cupboard containing emergency tools was also provided, and larger tools and a ladder were hung on racks attached to the bulkhead behind the driving cab. The trip and set lighting switch for the entire train was located on the inner bulkhead, but the two independent lights were controlled by switches adjacent to the doors,

A feature only found in the guard's van in early sets, and which was gradually removed, was a duct for ventilating the motors. These motors served fans in boxes attached to the ceiling of the guard's van, beneath two rectangular vents in the roof. No 5001 retained these until withdrawal but few others did, and the roof vents were removed and the roof flush plated.

The passenger accommodation was little changed from that in the later standard 4SUB sets. In each motor coach were eighty-two seats arranged in eight bays each, which seated ten in groups of three and two on each side. Between the seats was a passageway to allow passengers to circulate to find vacant seats, and when these were full to allow extra standing space. At the outer ends of the saloon and in each compartment were six seats. One of the two trailer cars was originally a saloon and the other a compartment coach, which could accommodate 102 and 120 seated passengers respectively. As some of the compartment vehicles were added from withdrawn augmented pre-war sets, there were some nine compartment trailers that seated only 110. The reason for the nine compartments instead of ten was that these vehicles were intended as composites and some compartments were wider to accommodate first class seating.

First class was discontinued in the London suburban area in 1941 and was not provided thereafter on trains that operated wholly within that area. Above every seat in the saloons was a luggage rack constructed from a tubular steel frame and originally incorporating a cord net. At the ends and in the compartments the luggage racks were supported on cast aluminium brackets with a varnished wooden pole securing the nets. The seats were of bench type with loose cushions, but with upholstered backs. Arm rests were rudimentary and only provided at the ends of the seating adjacent to the passageway and under the quarter-lights. The outward-opening doors were secured with a standard two-position spring-loaded catch; inside it was operated by a sliding catch in a chromed cast brass housing, but outside a T-shaped rotating brass handle was provided. The interior catch had an arrow symbol and the words 'To open' cast into the top. Adjacent to the outside handle attached to the body was a cast brass commode handle.

Door hinges protruded from the body and permitted an open door to lay back parallel to the body side. The interior of the door and panelling was finished in stained plywood. Ceilings were lined with white painted hardboard and the lights were exposed incandescent bulbs surrounded by a circular polished metal reflector, two per bay or compartment. As these were rated 70 volts, any that might have been stolen did not last too long in a 240 volt domestic supply! Sadly, however, this did not prevent occasional theft and damage. The end panels of the saloons and compartment panels above the seat backs were finished in a plastic laminate, on to which a mirror, flanked by two advertising frames of the same size, were attached. In each compartment only one mirror was provided, the other frame opposite frequently containing a

Front end detail on set No 5048, 6 February 1982. *Brian Morrison*

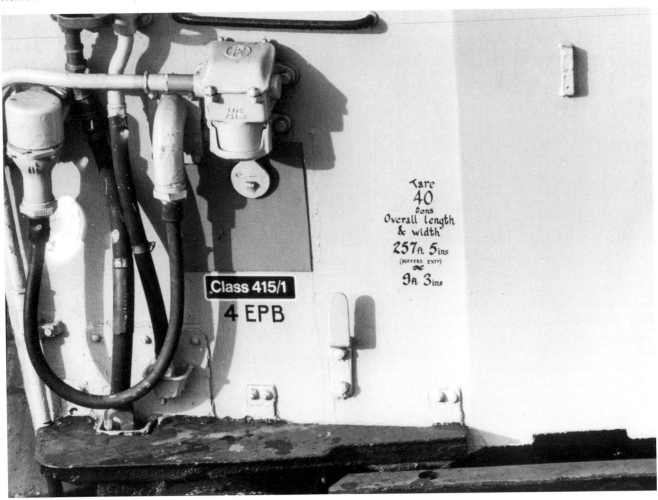

Interior '3+2' seating with aluminium luggage racks and a through gangway within the vehicle. This is from a refurbished unit with fluorescent lighting installed. *British Railways*

coloured map of the suburban area. Mirrors were etched with the letters 'BR'. Under the seats a metal grid protected the heaters but still allowed dirt to accumulate and could be quite unsightly. Floors were covered with linoleum.

In each door was a frameless drop light with a metal catch bar secured to the top. The words 'Press and pull down' were etched into the catch bar. Either side of the door was a fixed quarter-light, window, which was secured from the inside by a wood and mastic frame and was almost flush with the exterior body panel. The quarter-light glass was curved to match the shape of the body, and presented a very tidy appearance. Above the door inside was a recess containing the passenger communication cord and alongside it was a notice warning that improper use would incur a penalty of £5.

One non-adjustable ventilator was provided in the ceiling of each compartment or centrally above each seating bay. On the roof a 'torpedo' ventilator was provided at the corresponding position.

When introduced the livery was BR 'multiple unit green', not too far removed from Southern Railway 'malachite' green. Lettering and numbering was in 'straw' with black bordered Gill Sans typeface, and the BR emblem of a lion astride a wheel was applied to the motor coaches, facing towards the driving cab. The set number was placed above the route indicator, and was of the form 'S 5001 S', the coach numbers also bore an 'S' prefix and suffix. The body colour was continued to the continuous rain strip, which for the earlier sets was high up on the roof. The driving cab end was green too, but the inner ends were painted black, as was everything made of metal below the body. Roofs were originally grey, but discoloured rapidly to a muddy brown.

The roller blind route indicator consisted of white numerals on a black background and the letter shape, which filled half the indicator panel, was of a style that mimicked the shape of the older metal stencils. Above the twin numerals was a narrow blind that could, when necessary, display a white stripe. This stripe, when displayed, usually indicated that the train was running as empty coaching stock. Small handles were provided in the cab to adjust the display. Lighting was provided by six incandescent lamps inside a box that encased the indicator, and a door was provided from inside the cab so that the blinds could be checked and bulbs replaced.

The first set, No 5001, appeared in November 1951 and the last, No 5260, in January 1957. A total of 213 sets of this type were built during this period.

The coaches in the first two sets were originally numbered as a continuation of the 4SUB series. Thus set No 5001 was formed:

Motor Brake Third Saloon S8656S (underframe ex 8391)

Compartment Third S10398S ex 3SUB augmentation coach

Saloon Third S9035S (underframe ex 9526)

Motor Brake Third Saloon S8657S (underframe ex 8335).

And 5002 was formed:

Motor Brake Third Saloon S8658S (underframe ex 8254)

Compartment Third S10345S ex 3SUB augmentation coach

Saloon Third S9036S (underframe ex 9569)

Motor Brake Third Saloon S8659S (underframe ex 8406).

The carriages, however, were renumbered into a new series in March 1952, as follows:

5001, S14001S, S15001S, S15101S, S14002S

5002, S14003S, S15002S, S15102S, S14004S

Subsequent sets were delivered in blocks with new number as follows:

5003, S14005S, S15003S, S15103S, S14006S up to 5033, S14065S, S15033S, S15133S, S14066S

5034, S14067S, S15159S, S15134S, S14068S up to 5053, S14105S, S15178S, S15153S, S14106S

5101, S14201S, S15179S, S15154S, S14202S up to 5105, S14209S, S15183S, S15158S, S14210S

5106, S14211S, S15184S, S15234S, S14222S up to 5155, S14309S, S15233S, S15283S, S14310S

5156, S14311S, S15284S, S15334S, S14312S up to 5205, S14409S, S15333S, S15383S, S14410S

5206, S14411S, S15384S, S15394S, S14412S up to 5215, S14429S, S15393S, S15403S, S14430S

5216, S14431S, S15034S, S15404S, S14432S up to 5260, S14519S, S15078S, S15448S, S14520S

(*Unfortunately space does not permit a full listing of the numbers of the reused underframes to create the new vehicles. David Monk-Steele has kindly agreed to provide a full listing upon request.*)

Initially the first sets were delivered to the Western District to operate between Waterloo and Guildford. On 30 June 1952, fifteen sets were allocated to work the summer timetable, of which twelve were in traffic and three were spare, but by 15 September fourteen were required for the winter service.

Three more sets were allocated on 8 June 1953, and thirty-eight were allocated still to the Western District, with thirty-four required for the 1953 winter service from 21 September.

By 14 June 1954 twenty-four sets were allocated to the Eastern District for the commencement of the first phase of the 'ten-car scheme', with forty sets working Western District services and now with ten sets 'spare'. The Eastern District allocation had risen to thirty by the winter timetable commencing 20 September 1954, and spares increased to sixteen.

Again on the Western section, the unmistakable vista of Clapham Junction, No 5109 on a circular Waterloo–Brentford–Richmond–Waterloo working on the final leg of its journey, 18 September 1974. *Brian Morrison*

Unit No 5211 at New Cross with a Dartford Loop working, 28 November 1978. *John Chalcraft*

For the 1955 summer services from 13 June 1955 the Central District was now using fifteen sets, and the Eastern district allocation had risen significantly to seventy sets. To cater for this the Western district allocation was reduced to twenty-eight.

For the summer 1956 service there were 116 sets for the Eastern district services, fifteen for the Central, and twenty-eight for the Western. Only sixteen sets were kept spare. For summer 1957 all 213 sets were now allocated, 121 to Eastern district, 23 to the Central, 44 to the Western with 25 spare.

In October 1952 set 5001 had a fortnight working on the South London line as a trial towards the replacement of the former ex 'Brighton' AC stock, but this becomes part of the next chapter.

In the official Carriage Working Notice the 4SUB units were simply shown as '4'. To distinguish the new electro-pneumatic braked stock, the type code was altered to 4(EPB), later contracted to 4EPB. Although from a passenger perspective there was little difference between the trains, from an operating point of view if a 4EPB arrived to attach to a 4SUB instead of the booked 4SUB, the operational incompatibility was a distinct embarrassment!

Rebuilt
The Letters and Comments Pages

With the headcode indicating 'Train terminating at Portsmouth & Southsea' T9 No 116 waits departure from Fareham on the last leg of its journey, 2 July 1949. *Denis Callender*

Using the familiar phrase, 'a bumper bundle' again this time, so straightaway from Alan Blackburn.

'I hope the following may be of interest, Re *SW33*, and various comments in page order: p5 Charles Anderson. There were indeed three ways of working with Sykes on the South Western or London West as it was in my time – we are speaking of 1957.

'One of my first jobs as a signalman was at Grove Park on the Hounslow Loop. Here one worked normal Sykes SR Block Regulations to Chiswick when it was open, but the so-called "London Block" to Barnes when Chiswick was closed. "Call attention' was not used. When you had a train for Barnes you simply "Warned it on" with a train description, the signalman at Barnes then (usually) accepted it by repetition and cleared

the Sykes to "Free". More likely though he simply acknowledged your warning with one beat on the bell. When the train was approaching closely, you warned it again to Barnes. He might then accept it in the normal way but much more likely he would accept the train under Block Regulation 5 "Section clear, junction blocked" 3-5-5. This was repeated back to him, all at some speed I might add as you did not actually want to stop the train approaching, especially if it was a freight.

'There was also only one ordinary stop signal on the up line, and no warning arm. If you had timed all this correctly and your approaching train was still moving, you cleared the signal slowly and, as the book said, exhibited a steady green hand signal, and as the driver passed you bawled "Section clear junction blocked" at him as he went by. The box was very close to the track, close enough for the fireman of an up freight to lean up one day and steal one of the box cushions!'

Apropos Alan's comment about lowering the arm of the stop signal slowly as a means of communicating with the driver, this took skill on the part of the signalman and was also only possible with some mechanically worked signals – due to their distance from the box/the route taken by the operating wire, etc. I once had an old signalman tell me he continued the practice of slowly clearing the indication to 'off' after his signals were changed to colour lights – really!

'The third method, unofficial by this time but still used on the very busy Wimbledon and Richmond lines, was to give the "Train out of section signal" and then immediately give the box in rear a "Free" on the Sykes, knowing that if there was no train following there very soon would be. In effect this meant the signals were only "on" when they were actually protecting a train. In quiet times they reverted to normal working. I remember being told that this was the origin of the "Blocking back signals", only to be used when you needed to stop a train from leaving the previous box.

'P22 Cross Country working. In the early 1950s I was a box boy at Fratton West. I well remember that all the Bristol and Cardiff workings were formed of ex-GWR stock with Southern engines, D15s usually. All the local steam workings were formed of ex-LSWR non-corridor three-sets, usually strengthened with similar thirds. The engines were T9s, M7s, BR Class 4 2-6-0s, or SR Us. The 12.15 through train to Plymouth was formed with new BR Mk 1 four-sets, the engine a C2X or a Q1 as far as Fareham, both classes of engine being capable of a surprising turn of speed. Southern corridor stock of Maunsell or Bulleid origin was only rarely seen in Portsmouth at this time. All trains were worked by SR engines except for one of two services from Reading, which was hauled day in day out by *Littleton Hall*. The other Reading service was always hauled by an N15X. Summer weekends produced more *Hall*s or T9s. I well remember a T9 starting ten Midland coaches from a dead stand off the curve at Portcreek Jn, a slow job but he did not slip once. Incidentally Portsmouth and Southsea was never referred to as such, it was always called Portsmouth Town, its original name; one spoke of "down the Town" or "over the Harbour". To complete the local picture, the Dockyard goods was hauled by Els or a O2 that came redundant from Dorchester after the Portland branch closed. Shunting was done by E1s or E4. The Hayling was, of course, worked by Terriers, which normally did nothing else, although one did take a couple of oil cars over the harbour once and one might have shunted on the quay at Littlehampton.

'P45. The Terrier is either No 32677 or 32678 seen at Eastleigh in 1963, both were sold to Butlins and repainted in Brighton yellow livery, as you see. One can't be too sure which is which. No 32677, the one-time *Carisbrooke*, had MacLeod front footsteps but so far as I know never worked with a Drummond chimney, while 32678, one-time *Bembridge*, had a Drummond chimney but no front footsteps? I think my money is on 32678; that front footstep does not look like a Ryde job.

A Reading to Portsmouth Harbour working hauled by Basingstoke-based N15X No 32328 *Hackworth* waiting to leave Fareham on 11 June 1949. *Denis Callender*

'P49 etc. The photo of wagon S23682 is one taken at Ashford in 1948 of a Diagram 1369. For some reason an attempt was made in 1948–49 to photograph an example of every Southern wagon diagram. I do not know why this was done or if the job was ever completed but it must have taken some time. Each wagon was painted properly in SR brown for the occasion but I doubt that any other general repair wagon had this finish.

'Southern Railway photography. I was told that prior to the war the SR had no photographic staff. When a photograph was required a member of staff interested in photography was asked to do the job. The well-known photographer O. J. Morris took some official photos at Eastleigh and in the IOW. While over at Ashford a local photographic firm, D'arth and Condon, took a large number of pictures, including the wagon diagram job. It lost the business when one of its people became too familiar with the daughter of a senior member of the works staff. Otherwise, Topical Press took a lot of general photographs as required.

'All this changed with the outbreak of the Second World War when it became necessary to provide photographic evidence of bomb damage to the War Damage Commission in order to claim monies back from the government, I do not know the exact details. In this connection a photographic department was set up at Waterloo with, at its peak, one might guess that there were quite a large number of people employed. By the 1960s this was down to a small number and latterly in the 1970s only two or three. By the 1980s there was only one; John Goss, who later did BR work as a private individual.'

I have heard similar about the photographic department – at Eastleigh a Mr Marshall was involved, either him or, as Alan puts it, a member of staff with an interest in photography was used.

Now from Chris Sayers-Leavy:

'SW32 and the content of SW32. Another very interesting issue. I don't have much new information for you this time – and this letter is more a matter of personal "observations" really – well you did say that comments were always welcome.

'The letter from John Burgess. This was a very interesting read. I was already aware of the historical usage of "raised rail" crossings (indeed it had even been tried again in recent years as a temporary means of crossing over engineering trains/vehicles undertaking maintenance work in long double line possessions that no longer have crossings points in them). Generally this sort of crossing was used in slow-speed track layouts, yards, quarries and industrial premises. So to find that it had been used on what we now would call "running" lines is quite remarkable – not the least, because of the obvious risk of "fouling" the raised rails. Indeed, we do in fact have raised check rails in use today (that often derail slow speed road/rail engineering vehicles) but from the perspective of through running these are an aid to alignment rather than a potential derailment hazard.

'The benefits in construction costs of such a raised rail crossing are obvious, let alone before we consider (in modern terms) the problems caused by having a "break" in the through running rail. What I find almost unbelievable is the clearance dimensions quoted. This is not to say that I doubt in anyway John's reporting of the incident, rather more that our Victorian forebears could think that that such close tolerances were acceptable for the safe passage of trains conveying passengers? The amount of vertical movement undertaken by a locomotive as it travels along the track must have been known at the time. Add to this that loco springs could be prone to breaking – and you have completely removed the stated clearances on the Crampton loco. Even at 3in (measured, I am assuming, on a stationary loco or perhaps taken from a design drawing?) this is a very tight clearance that could easily be compromised in service at speed. This suggests a rather cavalier attitude by the operating company (SER?) but then it seems to have gone further and made matters worse by stating that "they have removed the 'ash pans' from the Cramptons remaining in service", as without some supplementary arrangement this would mean that hot ash and small pieces of coal that passed through the firebox grate would just be dropped onto the track, with the associate track/crossing fire risk.

'I am not aware of the captions that John refers to in the E. Wallis collection book-

Chris – shame on you, the 'Southern Infrastructure' books really are worth viewing, with numerous five-star Amazon reviews for each.

-but I would venture to suggest that the ramp shown was not for any specific "deflection" purpose, but is rather more it is "last chance" protection for anything that may be hanging loose on the underside of a train; i.e. broken brake pull rods, damaged pipes/safety chains and even 'stretched' three-link couplings, etc. [check out the lower picture of 15202 on p81 of SW32] and in a similar way even today "four foot" protrusions are often fitted with a ramp on their leading face in the direction of travel, i.e. AWS magnets and the like.

'Diesel shunters. The development of the internal combustion engine (ICE) as against the external combustion engine [i.e. steam engines] for railway applications is an interesting one that moved forward significantly in the 1930s. Not many people realise that Rudolf Diesel was not the "inventor" of the compression ignition heavy oil engine but his name has become synonymous with the modern derivative of this system as he brought together the various concepts into a practical working power unit in 1893. This was in a similar manner to the improvements that James Watt made to the steam engine. I believe that the first practical working shunting loco dated from 1896 and was used at the Woolwich Arsenal, but rail application progress after this engine was very slow.

'Early diesel engines tended to be big and heavy with a "long stroke" and as a consequence they were slow running by today's standards, with a narrow "power band", i.e. they were more suited to "fixed" as against "variable speed" applications and this in turn led to their typical uses being electricity generation in marine and stationary installations, and driving pumps or "line shafts", etc.

'Examination of the picture on p4 reveals a substantial rather "marine looking" vertical straight six-cylinder engine

In *SW34* Roger Simmonds wrote concerning the former signal box at Freshwater and lamented that he had been unable to find an image of the structure when later in use as a bus shelter. Fortunately that omission can now be resolved thanks to Tim Clarke, who has sent the attached view with the comment, 'Attached is a photograph taken by myself as a teenager in 1969 of the building with a collection of holidaymakers waiting for the next bus. As you can see, the door opening has been moved to the front left-hand side, in the same place as in its trackside days at Wootton, but not where it was on Freshwater station.' *Tim – thank you.*

with a relatively high centre of gravity, taking up 75 per cent of the available space. The crankcase hatches (the six rectangular holes) giving access to the connecting rod and "big end bearing" for each cylinder. Nevertheless, this type of engine turned out to be well suited to the tasks required of a diesel shunter with the weight of the engine and so on being a positive advantage in terms of adhesion/braking and rail head tractive effort. Compare the size of this stated six-cylinder English Electric engine developing 350bhp at 680rpm with the top picture on p90 – where the stated output of the Paxman twelve-cylinder RPH type engine is 500bhp at 1,250rpm – from an engine that would seem to be a fraction of the size of the engine in 15202? More on this later on.

'What might have been? This was a very interesting piece, and while I was not aware of the details before the proposal does not really surprise me. We should not forget that Tilling–Stevens, the bus builder and operator, was operating its "petrol electric" vehicles in what became Southern railway territory before the First World War. As the title suggests, this vehicle was basically a petrol-powered generating set mounted on a bus chassis. Hence the expanded term of "oil electric" for "compression ignition" engines that ran on what at the time was a by-product of the petrol/paraffin distillation process. The "oil" by-product was cheap and plentiful but without any definitive use. Rudolf Diesel changed this situation by producing a practical engine that could use this plentiful fuel source.

'There had been UK developments by Herbert Akroyd Stuart, who apparently at one point even considered coal dust as a fuel but settled on "heavy oil" as a fuel source in his hot bulb ignition engine (that have become known as "semi

diesels") but as detailed elsewhere diesel is the name that came to the fore for what was known as the heavy oil engine.

'The involvement of the engineering concern William Beardmore does not really surprise me either, however what I did not know until I did a bit of research was that the Glasgow-based company (William Beardmore) – had also built a number of steam locomotives in the 1920s for UK railway companies as well as overseas railways. Beardmore also produced its own diesel engines and apparently through a tie up with Canadian Westinghouse was involved in building "self-propelled" railroad cars – using diesel engines.'

The firm of William Beardmore was also a pioneer in attempting to sell diesel railcars to the GWR in the 1930s – see GWR Exposed by my good friend, Jeremy Clements, published Ian Allan.

'The origins of the drawing printed on p73 are not clear and it may well be a modern drawing produced to illustrate the concept being described? I would suggest that the depiction of an eight-cylinder diesel engine that would produce 600hp is very over-optimistic in terms of the physical size of such an engine in 1927!

'Diesel Shunter Finale: I agree that the concept of No 11001 as a dual purpose machine is something of a curiosity, but there again it is easy these days to forget the concept of "wagon load traffic" and all that went with it – pick-up freights and yard transfers etc – sixty-five years ago.

'Whilst the caption to the drawing on p87 refers to the "massive flywheel" this description is a little misleading as the text states that it is a "fluid coupling", sometimes referred to as a "fluid flywheel", the input and output shafts of which are not connected directly together (unless a lock up system is installed). This device uses the viscosity of the oil contained within it to provide a "limited slip" clutch arrangement. Such arrangements were common in London buses of the period and in other vehicles using constant mesh gearboxes. Just imagine trying otherwise to change gear on a railway engine with a "crash" gearbox! A similar system was used in the Drewry O2 class diesel shunters introduced by BR. These days a fluid coupling arrangement would be best described as being a "torque convertor".

'However, the main point here that I wanted to raise is the engine development that has taken place in the period between the Maunsell diesel electric shunters and the Bulleid diesel mechanical machine. This was a period of rapid development and improvement of diesel engines. The biggest problem with the compression ignition engine was getting the fuel to ignite and burn thoroughly in the cylinder. British engineer Harry Ricardo realised that the secret to this problem was the way in which the combustion air and the fuel mixed in the cylinder and developments in the late 1920s to '30s led to significant improvements in the efficiency and power output of "compression ignition" engines. Ricardo engineering is still very active in this area of engine development today. Other improvements also took place at the same time pushed on by the development of aircraft and road vehicles, notably supercharging (leading to turbocharging) and multi-bank engines. These developments are readily seen by the difference in size of the power units being referred to and their power outputs.

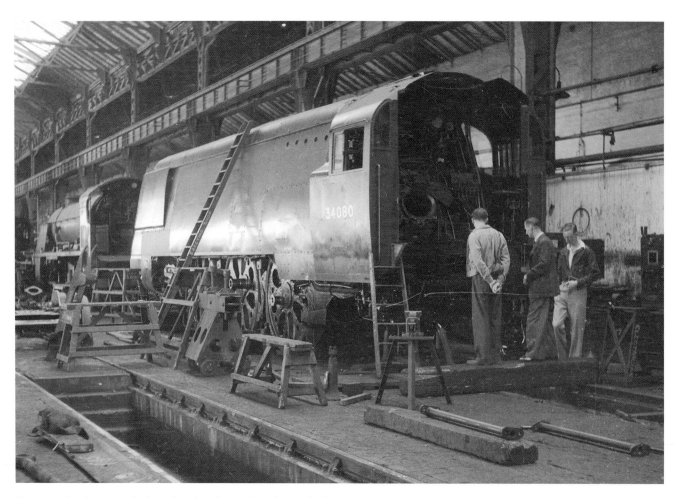

The name Ricardo Engineering from Shoreham featured heavily in Bulleid's work on sleeve valves. Nothing to do with the valves themselves but certainly to do with Mr Bulleid. Jeffery Grayer has submitted this image under the heading 'Birth of a Bulleid'. Jeffery continues, 'The as yet unnamed Battle of Britain Pacific seen nearing completion inside Brighton Works in 1948 is No 34080, later to bear the name and badge *74 Squadron*, one of twenty-four locomotives named after specific squadrons that took part in the pivotal 1940 battle. This example entered service on 20 August 1948 but was one of several members of the class never to have an official naming ceremony. Initially allocated to Ramsgate, it moved to what was only its second home at Exmouth Junction a decade later and was withdrawn from there in September 1964 having covered 750,000 miles in traffic. The three spectators are obviously interested in the cab but perhaps of greater note is the immaculate condition of the air-smoothed casing when new, a state that was seldom maintained under operational conditions. The engine remained in its original form until withdrawal and was scrapped at Birds of Morriston at the end of 1964. No 34080 was part of the fourth batch of twenty locomotives of this type ordered by the Southern Railway but not delivered until after nationalisation, the final batch of twenty not completed until No 34110 was delivered in January 1951. The actual 74 Squadron was part of the RAF 12 Group, operating both Spitfires and Hurricanes from, among others, Hornchurch, Kirton-in-Lindsay and Biggin Hill airfields, and was not disbanded until September 2000. Notice the locomotive number on the cabside, smaller than usual figures being used.

'The Paxman engines used the "V" form engine, a favourite form developed in America that allowed a very compact power unit to be built that also reduced the stroke length of the engine, which led to higher crankshaft speeds being possible. This compared with English Electric, which stuck to the "straight" form of "marine" type construction for its smaller "railway" engines. Interestingly, a similar "relative" development is still going on today, with some of the last Class 73 electro-diesel locos having their original English Electric engines replaced by modern 1,600hp units, thus turning them into even more versatile machines – and likely to become the most useful of all of the ex BR diesel locos that are in use today. A number of these locos have actually been purchased back from preservation for further mainline use and they can now be found in all parts of the UK, not just their former Southern homeland.

'Lastly on diesels, Mr Bulleid must certainly take first prize in one area – 11001 was one of the ugliest locos ever constructed for a main line operator.

Be careful Chris, there are an awful lot of Bulleid fans out there – as I know to my cost! Chris also has some views on issue No 34.

'The pictures on p89 and 90 of the Hither Green derailment of *253 Squadron*. I know nothing of the incident other than that which has been published previously, but what struck me in these pictures is that virtually everybody is wearing a hat of some kind, and that there is probably a hierarchy in the types of hat being worn. Viz: a bowler, a few trilbys, a number of flat caps, several berets and a number of "grease tops". Only one person is without a hat, from what I can see at a quick glance, and I would venture to suggest the following hierarchy:

The bowler – management
Trilbys – supervisors, known as inspectors at the time
Flat caps – the breakdown gang
Berets – fitters
Grease tops – MPD staff that have been sent over to assist
The individual without a hat is probably a member of office staff, maybe a P&T man.

'I also held the title of inspector as a lowly graded supervisor in the late 1970s (old habits die hard), although it was all about to change. By the early 1980s I was at Southern House as a "manager" and I had supervisors who reported to me, and they were all very reluctant to give up the title of inspector.'

I am corrected now by Peter Swift:

'The photo of (Winchester) Chesil station on P7 of *SW35* looked familiar. It is not a 28xx, which never ran with 4,000 gallon tenders. It is No 4925 *Eynsham Hall*, which should not be there at all, as it is a red engine. It was certainly the only time I saw a '*Hall*' on the DNS line. The date is 5 April 1961, No 4925 is waiting on the first of two portions of the train; the second portion was headed by 3835."

Speaking also of the Charles Anderson articles – thanks to many who have been most complimentary about this series of articles, I must though apologise for a gaffe that appeared in the final instalment in SW35. For some reason the name

'Worting Junction' was corrupted to 'Worthing Junction' and was not picked up until after publication. My thanks to those (several) who have pointed out the error.

Now to Jeremy Clarke:

'Re *SW35*, may I chuck in my 'two-pen'orth' to the various discussions. First though, the photo on p20: I've seen this before though searches through everything I've got to do with the S&D have failed to locate it. So far as I recall, the man holding the bell is Porter Mogg, who spent all his working life at stations on "The Branch" and particularly at Edington Junction (or Edington Burtle as it once was). It was, in earliest days, used to warn potential passengers of a train approaching.

'Now, Rebuilt and the Hastings 6S units. I have a slightly different version of events that produced them, though apparently from the same rolling stock source as quoted by your correspondent. Certainly short platforms were a consideration, but as I understand it, the original intention was that six-coach sets should be worked push/pull by a diesel engine of roughly the same dimensions as one of the coaches. In other words, seven vehicles had to be squeezed into a length the equivalent to six 'standard' coach lengths. It was only when the frames for the first batch of coaches had been constructed that this idea was shelved in favour of DEMU formations. To a degree the fact that the later 6L sets were produced and worked quite satisfactorily in and out of the ex-SER London termini might confirm this.

Not a million miles from Walton-on-Thames where the running trials of the 'River' tank were concluded abruptly, an unidentified Battle of Britain approaches Surbiton, Waterloo bound. *Arthur Taylor*

'As to their riding, the accident report into the Hither Green disaster certainly mentions the clearance difficulties that constrained some aspects of the bogies' design but it does not state specifically what that aspect was. (Southern Way Special 12 The Other Side of the Southern – a Further Selection *by David Monk-Steele and due to be released in the autumn of 2016 speaks in detail about this facet of the Hastings unit –Ed.)* Despite the narrowness of the bodies, it remained essential to ensure lateral movement was still restricted in the tunnels on the route south of Tonbridge. (S. C. Townroe once noted that after tracklaying in one of these tunnels, a slight misalignment – pre-diesel traction – caused all the door handles to be ripped off the carriages of two trains passing one another in it.) To that end there were hard rubber stops on the bogie frames designed to inhibit movement beyond the lateral maxima if the springs failed to do so. But that meant that on rough track, the sort produced by the continuous running of stock with heavy axle-hung motors, there was an unhealthy "biff" every time that lateral maximum was exceeded, with a consequent momentary stress on that bit of rail. The length of track north of Grove Park where the rail broke was, in my daily experience of it in the 1960s, pretty rough and on the few occasions I rode it in a Hastings DEMU I valued the rather less heart-stopping travelling of a Kent Coast 4-CEP. (The 2-HAPs could also be very lively at speed, especially the trailer if it was leading.)

'Then the "Rivers" – the "Rolling Rivers" – again the track was principally to blame. How else could No 890, the sole three-cylinder version classed K1, have reached 83½mph over the Great Northern main line with Nigel Gresley on the footplate yet, in the same series of tests, a K was reported to have scared him witless at Walton-on-Thames when travelling at nowhere near that speed, so much so the test had to be abandoned? Brighton men were well used to handling large tank engines and may perhaps have had rather better track on which to run the "Rivers" than pertained on the SER. Records of complaints from the former LBSCR appear to be less vocal or less common than those of the SER men. The ballast on its main line in 1927 was still Dungeness shingle bound with ash, hardly a satisfactory base for heavy and fast work. Yes, the Metropolitan bought its Woolwich bits with the intention of using them on freight work but when the LNER took over Met steam workings, there was no scruple on heading passenger services with them, something denied the Southern's W class because of the embargo placed by the chief civil engineer, George Ellson, who held the same position with the SECR and had had responsibility for the main line through Sevenoaks.

'Now, the vexed TC unit: only one 2BIL set was involved, No 2006, from, I believe, late-summer 1963 in a move to provide for increased peak hour demand on the Oxted line. Devoid of its shoes and power gear and with the former motor coach at the London end, it sandwiched five suburban trailers and was numbered 900. Power was provided by a class 33. There was never any intention of working push/pull despite there being driving cabs at both ends of the set. In 1966, in line with trailer unit convention, it was reclassified 7TC and renumbered 701. Following withdrawal in 1969 the 2BIL was broken up but the trailers found further use in 4SUB and 4EPB units. (I used to see the set regularly at Norwood Junction as its usual down working at one time was the 17.20 London Bridge–Tunbridge Wells West.)

'May I add another bit for Rebuilt regarding the upper photo on p30? The caption mentions the engine working hard from a signal check, a view supported by the fact the sands are working. But what is perhaps more interesting is the second van in the train. It is one of the three built at Ashford in 1936 for the Night Ferry and numbered simply "1–3". The roof line is of the usual ex-SECR ellipse but much shallower to provide sight through the central raised guard's lookout required by French regulations. A communication cord passed over the roof and had to clear the lookout by means of rods and cranks. The guard's doors were opposite one another but inset by 4½in, meaning they uniquely opened inwards. The vans were fitted with safety chains – another French requirement – electrically lit and dual brake fitted, those necessary fittings taking up so much space beneath the floor, the lighting batteries had to be placed in one of the two luggage compartments.

'Other than during the war years they ran daily in the Night Ferry, two being in service, one spare, until 1960. The Westinghouse equipment, safety chains and communication cords were removed then and all three were repainted from the dark blue livery of the ferry cars into Southern Green. The lighting remained for some years longer but with that removed they were regarded as ordinary luggage vans. It is clearly in this guise the pictured van is working. Nos 1 and 2 were withdrawn in 1969 but No 3 soldiered on until July 1974. None survives.'

My own sleight at modern day political correctness (editorial in *SW35*) drew a response from Rod Garner:

'Your piece about our friend Thomas reminded me of the book we have just bought for our grandson, the title being *The Lost Puff*. In it Thomas is incapacitated when playing games and bumping into Toby. The water in his tanks, "... sloshed all over Thomas and put out the fire in his COMBUSTION CHAMBER'!" This expression is repeated twice more. From the addresses on the back of the book, I guess that the text has been translated several times. Not really *Southern Way* material, but, well, you started it.

Guilty as charged M'lud

Rod spent much of his career in the Insurance industry and adds the following anecdote as proof of the difficulty in sometimes dealing with clients:

'This reminds me of the technical specification I had once in connection with a claim. When in the engineering insurance business, a piece of machinery was described as a "water sheep". It turned out to be a hydraulic ram ...'

Rod also points out that in *SW36* my excuse for including an illustration of an LNER pigeon van was that it probably contained SR pigeons – now why didn't I think of that!

Several readers, including Colin Chambers and Roger MacDonald, have also pointed out the error in a caption from one of Jim Seddon's views. To quote Roger:

An up West of England express approaching Locke King Bridge, just west of Weybridge station, probably about 1956 or so – a favourite location for Frank Foote. The loco appears to be Battle of Britain No 34063 *229 Squadron*. The formation is a little unusual in that the catering vehicles are at the front of the train rather than in the middle, so this is possibly a service that has come through from the 'far west' to Exeter already formed of the rear seven coaches, or perhaps from Exmouth/Sidmouth/Seaton and has had the front three coaches added at either Exeter Central, Sidmouth Junction or Seaton Junction. The coaches are: a Maunsell 1936 open third in crimson and cream, tavern composite restaurant and tavern car, again in crimson and cream, then a pair of Maunsell 1930/33 open thirds, one in green, the other blood and custard, then a Bulleid multi-door three-set in green with two more unidentified – perhaps a Bulleid or Maunsell two-set on the rear. Unfortunately there is no exact date, but at a guess the time is early to mid-afternoon on a summer Saturday. If the loco is No 34063, then allocated to Nine Elms, she is returning home after a trip westwards earlier in the day. *Image Frank Foote, caption notes by Mike King*

'It was good to see a new take on the last year of Southern steam through the photos of Jim Seddon. The shot on the top of p33 of a BR Standard 2-6-0 is not, I think, a Class 4. The shape and height of the chimney gives it away as belonging to a Class 3, the well-known 77014, a loner on the Southern Region and shedded at Guildford. Its relatively clean condition is probably because two days later it worked the LCGB's Dorset & Hants Rail Tour.'

Former Eastleigh fireman Keith Dawe's name has already been mentioned earlier in this issue and he now provides an interesting aside to the photographic article on the 'Salisbury Goods' at Chichester (Issue 35):

'This piece evoked memories of the same working in the 1960s when I was firing at Eastleigh. I worked this turn several times and it was always a substantial load. By then the allocated power was a "Standard 5" and it was worked by Salisbury men as far as Eastleigh and Eastleigh men from thence to Chichester.

It was always known to loco crews as the "Chi Goods". At the period that I was familiar with the working, it did not call in at Eastleigh as was suggested, but a crew change was made there. As it was a lengthy train and would foul all four main running lines as it straddled the junction *(from the Chandlers Ford line)*, the changeover was effected on the move.

'The Salisbury men were already ready to vacate the engine as she swung in to the down local platform from the Romsey line and the Eastleigh men would position themselves at the extreme London end of that platform – then Platform 4. With the train moving at a brisk walking pace, the Eastleigh driver would jump aboard, followed by his fireman. A brief verbal handover would take place that included information about the load and the make-up of the train, vacuum head and how well she was steaming – or otherwise – and then the Salisbury crew would vacate the footplate, hopefully before we ran out of platform!

'A similar changeover would take place with the guard. The only problem now was that the guard was a long way back and the train was on an "S" bend as it headed towards the Fareham line and with the driver's view further blocked by the usually full carriage sidings. Hence, he had no idea what was happening on the brake van.

'It was a question of just keeping the train moving at about the same pace until the van eventually swung around the corner on to the long straight past Tipton Yard, where hand signals were exchanged and the journey began in earnest.

'Your contributor is quite right in that we came off the train in the reception road at Chichester (Chi) and went light to Fratton Loco – tender first. At that time, I seem to recall the triangle was still in situ at Chichester but not in use. Anything coming to the yard from the east would at that stage be either diesel or electric hauled, so we were probably the only steam engine needing the facilities. As my driver would say; there was quite often "one of them new-fangled electrical things" in one of the electrified sidings, possibly waiting to take over any ongoing part of our train.

'Again, from memory, we would square up the engine at Fratton and leave her on the pit road while we had our break, then work another loco – usually a "Woolley" or sometimes a "standard" over to Portsmouth Town and work a van train back to Eastleigh.

'It was actually while working the Chi goods one day that we had a bit of excitement. We had No 73089 on that occasion and all was well until we got midway between Fareham and Porchester, when she decided to drop the complete set of front firebars – together with my fire – into the ash pan. We had to alert the signalman at Porchester in the approved manner of a note tied to a knob of coal and lobbed at the box. We put the train away into Cosham yard and beat a hasty retreat to Fratton Loco while we still had enough steam to go and, more importantly, to stop. By the time we got the engine over the pit road the ash pan was welded solid and in no way was it going to open for me to clear out the fire and firebars. So there we left her and there she stayed for quite a while before she was put to rights and returned to traffic again.'

Sadly I have to report that the author of the article concerned, Stan Watkins, passed on in April 2016 and so never saw his article in print. We did ensure a copy was sent to his family.

___

Now from Peter Tatlow:

'I thought readers might be interested to learn that the photograph of LSWR No 297 at Waterloo reproduced on p25 (*SW32*) was taken by Archibald C. Johnstone on Saturday, 23 August 1913 when at the head of the 2.55pm to Southampton. This was just one of several photographs he took that day including at St Pancras, Kings Cross and Waterloo Jct. These and many others at London termini with a few in the Home Counties in 1913 and 1914 have been the subject of a series of eight articles in the late lamented journal *Railway Archive*, Nos 43 to 50. As well as No 297, *RA* 50 includes T9 No 720, L12s, T14s, H15s, L11s and an A12; while the SECR and LBSC are featured in issues 47 and 44.'

I would agree entirely, RA will be sadly missed.

Apart from the advantages of Rebuilt in giving readers the opportunity to air their own views, it also gives us the opportunity of using odd images that might otherwise never have an outing. One example is shown here (and with apologies for the scratches on the negative). An early design GWR railcar (the original 'flying banana' rail vehicle) seen about to enter Southampton Central tunnel. What it was doing at Southampton we cannot be certain, although two possibilities come to mind. The first was a special working for OURS (the Oxford University Railway Society), which was known to visit far and wide and with unusual 'motive power' on occasions. The second was a trial over the DNS line with a view to using this type of vehicle for certain services. (We know for sure such a test did take place in 1947 but the image seen here is not dated.) What we also know is the difficulty the (G)WR had in persuading the Southern authorities to allow the vehicle to run over SR metals. The SR was not satisfied the vehicle had sufficient weight or presence to operate track-circuits, which would appear strange as there had never been any such reservations by the home region.

Now from 'Windy' Gale:

'I read my Southern Way in batches due to the ("excessive" as my wife calls it) number of magazines and books that I buy every week, I have only just this morning got around to reading No 31 and was immediately struck by the query on P6 about the use of "Sidley" on a roof board. I do not know if this is the answer but it does have a sort of possibility of being the reason why a village should be shown on a roof board when all the other places are towns. Bear with me a minute while I give you a potted history of my reason.

'Back in the years just after the Second World War almost all my family were members of the St John Ambulance Brigade. My younger sister and I were cadets and my mother was a nursing cadet officer. Each year for a number of years, possibly from 1947 to 1951–52, we would attend the annual cadet camp at a large, specially prepared field site near Sidley in Sussex. One year we went by lorry but normally all our cadets from our divisions would go by train. Now, our camp was for the whole of the London District and to me, at that time, only 7 to 10 years old at the most, there seemed to be hundreds of us in camp at the same time. We would get a train from somewhere in the London area (probably Victoria or Charing Cross/London Bridge. I cannot for the life of me remember which but we lived close to the Hayes line so CX or Ldn Bdg is most likely) and having travelled up to this London terminal station we would be ushered on to the platform and herded into dedicated carriages by our leaders.

'Now if you can imagine a couple of hundred school kids with bags galore in SJAB uniforms along with some necessary camping gear trying to get into a very heavily loaded Saturday holiday train while the leaders tried to ensure that not only did we not lose anyone, but that they all got into the right carriages, a bit like evacuees of a few years before, I should imagine that the sight of a guiding carriage board with "Sidley" clearly marked on it would probably save a few heart attacks.

That way at least the first difficulty was overcome as we were at least mustered into carriages where we would be in the right place to transfer to the branch train at Crowhurst for Sidley.

'I believe the branch train at Crowhurst was formed up just across the platform from the train down from London, so being correctly positioned in the London train to be opposite the branch line train in a long platform would be another reason why the SR wanted to see that we got into the correct carriages in the first place. The only thing I remember about the situation at Crowhurst was that I thought the branch line train to Bexhill West was made up of "quaint coaches" and I vaguely seem to remember that the end of that train possibly had windows in it, a bit like our Hayes trains, so it might have been a pull-push unit.

'At Sidley we all alighted and formed up on the platform before carting our bags and boxes up the stairs to the road, which was at a higher level than the platforms. Then somehow we all trudged up the mile or so to the cadet camp situated on the Ninfield Road, which was a definite welcome sight after a long walk with heavy bags. I believe we may have borrowed trolleys or platform luggage trucks to carry the heaviest baggage so they must have been returned after our arrival because we almost certainly would not have had the old "Scouts" type handcarts. The camp site was under canvas bell tents but there were two brick buildings on the site, one for a mess hall and the other as a recreation hall should the weather be constantly wet. The site must have been permanent but they were brick buildings not Nissen huts, so whether they were pre-war or perhaps reused wartime military facilities I have no idea.

'Looking at the carriage roof boards, which I probably could not see from the platform anyway, being so short, it would make sense to have the word "Sidley" included on the roof boards of the carriages allocated to our group, even if only for that Saturday morning train that was also used by normal holidaymakers.'

Unfortunately we could not find anything specific to accompany 'Windy' Gale's piece but we did find this for Peter Hoare's letter. 6S unit No 1002 with a special Tunbridge Wells and Hastings working at the commencement of DEMU working, May 1957.

Now from Peter Hoare, who signs himself as 'Former Train Driver, Norwood Depot' The topic is that of certain Southern Region rolling stock:

'I have read the contribution to Rebuilt in the July 2016 edition of *The Southern Way* by Chris Sayers-Levy with great interest.

'No doubt better informed and wiser sources than I have already risen to the challenge of responding to Chris's points and questions but I hope the following may be of some additional value.

'Hastings 6S Units. The issue of why the first tranche of Hastings Line (6S) DEMUs were built on 57ft underframes is an intriguing one. According to some sources, the original plan was to have steel-bodied hauled stock as a "like for like" replacement for the existing "0" restriction coaches operating over the line but towed by diesel locomotives. What type and from whom it was intended to source these machines is, unfortunately, not specified. Perhaps an early version of a Crompton or something similar?

'To accommodate a twelve-car train with diesel loco attached within the available length respectively of platforms 5 and 6 at Charing Cross (not Cannon Street), taking into account adequate sighting of the departure signals, the coaches needed to be no longer than a "short" underframe allowed.

'The story goes that Eastleigh had already started to assemble the coaches based on 57ft underframes supplied by Ashford when the diesel loco concept was abandoned in favour of self-contained on-board power units in the form of the EE 4SRKT lump (rated at 500hp) operating through 250hp traction motors, resulting in a hasty revamp to produce two DMBSs for each six-car rake.

'With the length restriction and need to accommodate a loco in the consist removed there was no longer any reason to build the later tranches (6L and 6B) on shorter underframes and they duly emerged as "standard" length vehicles.

'I have to say it all sounds a tad apocryphal to me. For example, would it not have been necessary to accommodate two locos in each of the designated platforms at Charing Cross? One heading the incoming service and the other to take it away. Also, assuming something along the lines of a Crompton was envisaged as the motive power source, I imagine it might have been quite a struggle to haul twelve coaches single-handedly over certain sections of the route, especially in winter when train heating would have been required.

'Having worked in the railway industry perhaps nothing should come as a surprise and these factors may well have been considered, if not acted upon, as part of a larger thought process. However, I would suggest that a more likely explanation is that 57ft underframes were available, the stock was needed urgently because of some financial, political or operational imperative – or a combination of all three – and so the trains got built in their shortened form.

'Now to TC Stock. Two types of TC stock operated over the East Grinstead line: 6TC, which was designed to work with Crompton D6580 as a test bed for the genuine Trailer Control

No doubt taken on the same occasion, 'the great and the good' having dismounted from the special now make their way to inspect units and facilities at the new Bexhill DEMU maintenance shed.

At the rear of the shed, the first of the new 6S units, No 1001, on the left and with cables connecting it to the mobile testing unit on the right.

system (as applied to the 3TC and 4TC units used following the Bournemouth Line electrification), and 7TC which, although assigned to the Trailer Control series, was never modified to run in this mode. It is the latter to which I believe Chris was referring.

'The 7TC stock comprised the DMBS and DTC from 2BIL unit 2006 at the outer ends (with traction gear removed from the DMBS) and five former 4SUB intermediate trailers. The excellent Blood and Custard website (www.BloodandCustard.com) has a highly informative piece on the consist and history of the unit that really cannot be bettered.

'The modernised 3H Unit. Blood and Custard also provides detailed information on the "modernised" 3H unit No 1111 (subsequently 205 205). At one time it was intended to convert all the remaining DEMU stock in a similar fashion but, in the end, only three 3D (207) units were dealt with (and, unlike No 1111, without any attempt to make them operationally compatible with EMU stock apart from some minor circuit modifications to accommodate the insertion of a former 4CEP TSO in the consist in place of scrapped NDTCs). Although primarily intended to serve the Ashford to Hastings Marshlink route, they and No 1111 all put in appearances on Uckfield Line services from time to time. They were not popular with passengers and performance always seemed to be on the sluggish side compared with other units.

'The star of the remaining fleet was undoubtedly No 207 017. This former 3D unit – reduced to a two-car formation – was internally unmodified so retained tungsten lights and original upholstery, although it did get an external repaint into Connex South Central livery sometime in the early part of 2000. It earned

the sobriquet "Thrust II" – no doubt bestowed upon it by some wag of a driver – but boy did it go and, by DEMU standards, was something akin to a Deltic among Class 40s. I wonder if it runs as well in preservation on the Spa Valley Railway?'

My personal 'Bucket List' feature in *SW35* (dealing with the fate of No 35004) has drawn comments in two areas. Firstly from Nigel Tilly, who comments:

'Thanks for the article in Issue 35. The question of exactly what did happen has long fascinated me and I await eagerly responses to the issues raised.

'There is one question you pose, however, that I can answer. Tender No 3113, which was with No 35004 from 1944 until the time of the incident, currently sits in the National Railway Museum in York behind the sectioned No 35029. I called in at the museum and checked the tender number plate, which is still in position (the caption that goes with the loco at York describes it as a 6,000 gallon tender, and so presumably this has been incorrect for the entire time that the loco has been in the museum).

'In *The book of the Merchant Navy Pacifics* it shows a three-way tender swap took place in October 1965. No 3113 from 35004 went to 35029; No 3129 from 35029 went to 35011; and No 3121 went (nominally at least) from 35011 to 35004. From this one might assume that No 3129 from 35029 had a problem that was dealt with but that tender No 3121 from 35011 had a more serious problem that led to it being set aside for scrap with 35004. The remaining question therefore is, "What happened to tender 3121?"'

Any suggestions would be welcome.

I was hoping others might add their own personal bucket list, or more accurately perhaps bucket wishes, and we have received several. Jeremy Staines refers to the Bulleid Tavern Cars and also Bulleid's solitary sleeping car, while Terry Cooper speaks of various signalling queries that might now never be resolved. Nearer to home, my good friend Malcolm Snellgrove has long puzzled over where the corrugated goods shed at Fawley originated. He knows it was from one of three stations on the Meon valley line – but which one?

Chris Sayers-Leavy adds his own memories and also some wishes:

'I am not by nature a regretful person and very much a pragmatist, and therefore I cannot really say that I am "regretful" about any opportunity that I missed to see more "steam" than I did. My circumstances at the time, just leaving school and not yet earning more than my paper round money (15 shillings a week as I remember it), very much dictated the extent of any travelling that I could do to get to where steam was still being used. I lived at West Wickham on the Mid-Kent line to Hayes, which was electrified between the wars, so locally the only steam to be seen was the pick-up goods, which actually only really brought loaded wagons to the local coal merchants and took the empties back with it. These trips all finished or were turned over to diesel operation in the early 1960s. So my opportunities were then limited by how far I could cycle to the nearest activity.

'My parents did not really approve of these cycling trips, although my father introduced me to the delights of a steam engine by taking me down to the station coal yard on a Saturday morning to watch the yard being shunted (at a very early age). So I ventured to Orpington to see the last of the Kent coast steam but this soon finished. In the opposite direction was the Brighton mainline, electrified in the 1930s, so it was only the occasional excursion working/ECS and van trains or shunting in the yard. But there were the East Grinstead and Uckfield lines, albeit both now being worked by diesel units but with some steam workings to be seen and once you got to Oxted there were the regular Tunbridge Wells West services worked by the H class 0-4-4T locos. This was virtually all there was to be seen locally. Trips to London concentrated on the mainline stations and I did not even get to see the Kensington shuttle from Clapham Junction.

'However, in 1967 when my interest in steam was waning, a friend passed his driving test and using his mother's car we were able to venture across to the SW mainline, going to Raynes Park on one of the "racing sections" where the fast trains could be seen in full flight and on occasions to Surbiton. Right at the end, I had saved up enough money up for a steam trip to Weymouth and back. I also had family holiday opportunities in Bournemouth, Hayling Island and the Isle of Wight, and I managed to get to both the Isle of Wight and

Hayling Island again "under my own steam", so to speak, a few times before steam finished there/the line was closed.

'Of course, I would have like to have seen more; an unaccompanied trip to stay with relatives in Glasgow in 1962 for two weeks was quite enlightening and an unexpected thrill but other than that I rather just accepted that I was "born too late". Even so, with a whetted appetite I did then spend the next ten years after steam finished on BR involved in railway preservation, starting with the ill-fated Westerham line where the burgeoning M25 soon put paid to that scheme.

'What would I have liked to see? Well, probably the S&DR but it was just too far away from me. I would also have liked to see some of the main Works. I got into Swindon when they were reconditioning the "Adams" radial tank for the Bluebell, before it closed. I would also have liked a better camera and the wherewithal to take more/better pictures than I did with my Brownie 127. But all in all I'm just grateful that I saw what I did see rather than not to have seen it at all.'

Last but by no means least in so much as received correspondence is concerned, a note from Eric Youldon courtesy of Keith Chrystal:

'Eric Youldon has asked me to contact you regarding comments we have made about *SW34*. We both noted that on p60 No 30918 is actually No 30913. On p61 we considered the S15 was more likely to be a late King Arthur, between 30793 and 30806. If you look at an S15, the centreline of the driving wheels lines up with the lower edge of the outside cylinders, whereas on the larger wheeled Arthurs the centreline is in line with the piston rod, as would be expected with the 28in cylinders on both classes. On p63 the N1 is a U1 because No 1822 had a standard N class tender and the other five had similar but larger straight-sided tenders. Finally, on p18 the cars shown I believe are Opels (German Vauxhalls), so they are imports.'

Finally, we should add that *SW* had a mention in *The Times* recently. (In the *SW* office we do not aspire to such things). It occurred on 12 August when regular *SW* reader Brian Simmons wrote to the newspaper concerning an earlier piece. This earlier piece referenced communication between and the possibility of a tunnel linking the Isle of Wight with mainland England. Brian was quick to point out that an article on the proposed Solent Tunnel had appeared in *SW29*. Many thanks to Brian for his mention of *SW* in 'the paper of record' and also to Tony Atkins for spotting it in the first place.

Further, but all appreciated, contributions have been held over for no other reason than lack of space.

The South Eastern section is often the poor relation in *SW* but hopefully that is slightly addressed here with this delightful image of a pristine R1 No 31107 posed in Folkestone Yard.

Hills of the South

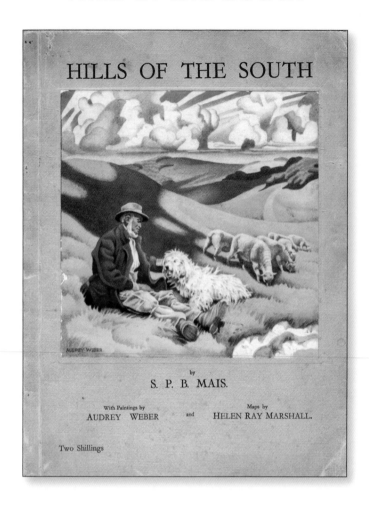

Jeffery Grayer recalls the 1939 Southern Railway-sponsored publication Hills of the South, written by the well-known author and broadcaster, S. P. B. Mais

Born in 1885, Stuart Petrie Brodie Mais' radio broadcasts for the BBC (in the 1920s and '30s, and during the wartime years of the early 1940s) made him a household name. He had even presented a 'Letter from America' some thirteen years before the more famous programme of the same name was fronted by Alistair Cooke. He was dubbed the 'Ambassador of the Countryside' for his series _This Unknown Island_, which popularised the English landscape among the general public. In addition to newspaper journalism and broadcasting he wrote more than 200 books ranging from travel, history and topography to literary criticism, autobiographies, spy stories and books for children.

At the age of 45, and having been made redundant for a second time from _The Daily Telegraph_ and with family responsibilities, he took the step of becoming a freelance writer. Among a variety of rather odd assignments, through which he financed among other things his summer holidays, he tried his hand at writing advertising copy for railway companies. This proved to be more lucrative than his books,

the Southern Railway also paying him a fee to accompany its ramblers on walks in the countryside. As Maisie Robson says in her biography of Mais, 'He would stride up hills declaiming like a TV historian as his flocks of off-duty clerks and shop assistants scurried along in his wake. The enthusiasm was real enough, paid or unpaid he was passionate about England.'

One of Mais' more notable excursions involved three trains, carrying some 1,300 passengers, which steamed into Steyning station, on the Shoreham-Horsham branch line, between 2 and 3 o'clock in the early hours of the morning of 17 July 1932. The walkers had come to witness the sunrise over Chanctonbury Ring, a nearby highpoint of the South Downs. As one incredulous observer commented, 'Such a performance can be witnessed free of charge 365 times a year with an extra matinée every fourth year. Are these people mad? For close on an hour I stood outside Steyning railway station watching the crowd decant themselves into the night.'

The cover image of _Hills of the South_ shows a shepherd with his rather unusual canine companion, an Old English sheepdog rather than the more usual Welsh black and white variety. This was apparently the only one of its kind to be found on the South Downs used for this work, the author encountering the shepherd on his ramble from Arundel to Worthing.

'SPB', as he was known colloquially, led the straggling column of mixed humanity from Steyning station towards the Downs, carrying both a hat and cap in one hand and an overcoat over the other arm. At no time during the long walk was he seen to wear any of them! In the train on which he travelled, he had visited every compartment and made friends with more than 400 people, and during the walk he hurried backwards and forwards like a sheepdog harrying his flock. Mais himself mentions this expedition in his *Hills of the South* when describing a new walk beginning at Steyning. He recalls that the last time he started a walk from Steyning station was in midsummer to see the moon set and the sun rise in the company of 1,330 or 1,440 fellow wayfarers. Although he recounts that they enjoyed themselves hugely, he remarks wryly that they saw neither the down-setting of the moon nor the uprising of the sun, experiencing instead a chilly, damp dawn that made 'enjoyment a matter of determination rather than of instinct.'

In 1939 the Southern Railway published the aforementioned *Hills of the South*, which featured a number of walks in the southern counties of West and East Sussex, Surrey and Kent, all, of course, served by trains of the SR. The book was illustrated by a number of colour maps drawn by Helen Ray Marshall, a poster artist and illustrator, and colour plates taken from paintings by Audrey Weber (1898–1981), who exhibited extensively at the Royal Academy, the Society of Women Painters and the New English Art Club. She worked for the SR as a poster designer and illustrator but in spite of her obvious ability surprisingly little is known about her. It is interesting to read this guide today nearly eighty years on from when it was written not only for the descriptions of the landscapes, much of which has changed out of all recognition, but for references to railway stations, many of which are no longer with us.

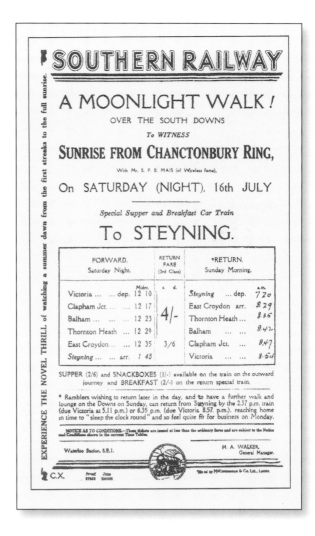

The map of the border country between Hampshire and West Sussex showing the operational Petersfield–Pulborough railway with the intermediate stations of Rogate for Harting, Elsted, Midhurst, Selham, Petworth and Fittleworth, all of which were to be swept away in 1955. The former Midhurst–Chichester line is no longer shown at this date as it had closed four years earlier in 1935, although the names of former stations at Cocking, Singleton and Lavant are still apparent. Bramber and Steyning on the former Brighton–Horsham line are also shown.

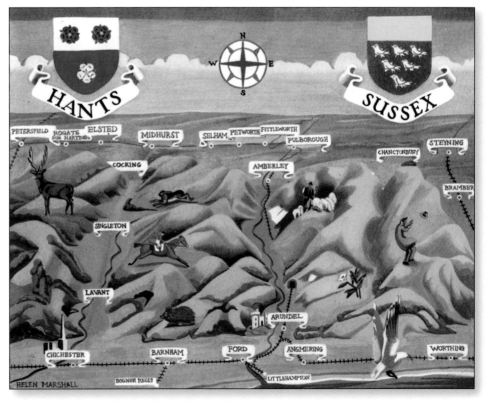

'SPB' begins his preface written from his rather quirky address of Toad Hall, Shoreham-by-Sea. by extolling the virtues of the hill country of the south. Gilbert White, the famous naturalist from Selborne, rather overdid the description by referring to the chalk downs of the south as 'that chain of majestic mountains …' Mais admits that there are no hills topping 1,000ft in the south, which does not therefore qualify them to be described as mountains, but height alone does not prevent each from having far reaching views and he opines that there are 'at least a thousand hills within 50 miles of London where no motorist can penetrate and man can be alone with Nature'.

As a prelude to his walks, he generally arrives at the local station by train wherever posssible, bearing in mind, of course, that this is a Southern Railway publication! Walk No 1 from Rogate to Midhurst begins thus … 'I set out on this journey southwards from Rogate station. The first village I came to was South Harting, lying snugly under the lee of the South Downs.'

After a walk taking in Beacon Hill, Didling Hill, and Cocking Down he comes to 'A high railway embankment hiding the flint walled Crypt Farm from view and on the other side of this embankment the stream became a watercress bed and almost immediately afterwards I was in the village of Cocking.'

Unfortunately, with the closure of the railway through Cocking a few years before the date of his ramble he perforce had to use Shanks' pony to reach Midhurst where he 'admired the deer park of Cowdray together with the ruins of the old castle before catching my train home.'

Another walk began from Petworth and ended at Pulborough, while another circular walk commenced from Arundel. 'When I got out of the train at Arundel Station on the February Sunday morning the sun was just breaking through the scurrying cloud' and terminated here but not before our intrepid walker had 'climbed the steep High Street where I found an excellent tea-place called Honeybuns, run by a French woman, before regaining my train at Arundel Station.'

Reminiscing about his guided walk from Steyning station back in 1932, he sets out again from this station to end his trek at Amberley. 'I was in an electric train at Amberley having spent 4½ hours of golden sunshine on the quiet hill tops without encountering a single motor car or a single walker and only four horsemen (hopefully not of the apocalypse variety!).'

Other stations mentioned in the book include Shoreham-by-Sea, Hassocks, Lewes, Brighton, Bishopstone, Polegate, Faygate, Balcombe, Wye and Sandling Junction, all thankfully still with us, although one feature of the latter station has long gone …

Cocking Station seen in the 1960s before conversion to a desirable residential property. By the time of Mais' ramble in 1939 only goods were handled here, the passenger service between Chcichester and Midhurst having ceased in 1935.

The Surrey map shows the former Guildford–Horsham line stations of Cranleigh and Bramley and Wonersh, lost in the Beeching cuts of the mid-1960s.

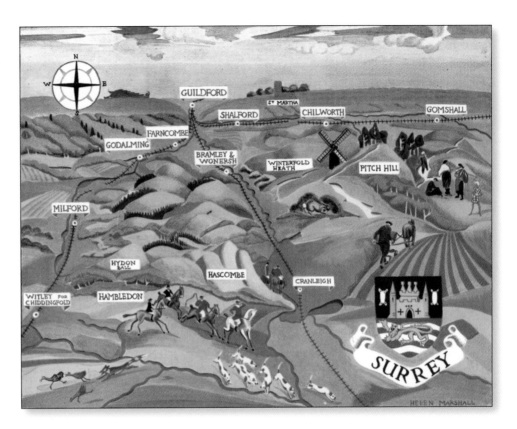

'I was over the brow looking down on the quiet park of Sandling on my right and the equally quiet station of Sandling Junction just below me. As I had half an hour to wait for my train I looked around for some place to have tea. During the whole of the day's walk, except at Etchinghill, I had passed no place of refreshment at all, and there isn't one at Sandling Junction. In my hunger I nearly broke into the camping coach that nestled in the siding.'(Camping coaches at Sandling featured in *SW35*).

Two of the walks begin from Cranleigh station on the former Horsham– Guildford line and in spite of hopes that the line from Guildford could be electrified and retained as far as Cranleigh, when closure plans were being discussed, unfortunately the whole line was closed in 1965. Mais' description of starting a walk from Cranleigh recalls a less hurried age …

'When I got out of the train at Cranleigh station there were rifts in the clouds and a general feeling of spring in the air. The ticket-collector told me that I couldn't miss my way to the hills, but in

A stylised rendition of the 480ft Mount Caburn near Lewes, which features on its summit the remains of an Iron Age hill fort.

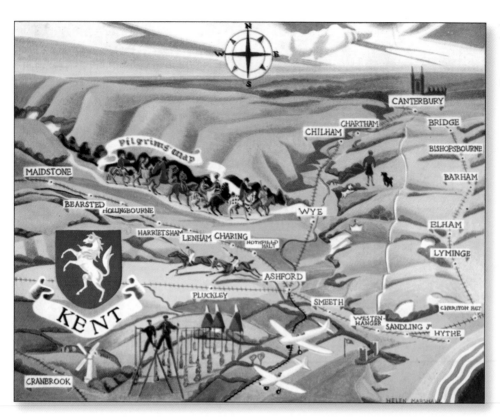

The map of Kent shows the Elham Valley route, the former branch to Hythe and Cranbrook station on the Hawkhurst branch, all casualties of progress.

spite of his coming out into the station yard to direct me between the two banks on the opposite side of the road I did miss my way.'

One could hardly imagine any ticket collector doing this today! *(Especially as it would mean asking a machine of the type that appears ever hungry and willing to gobble one's ticket at the first opportunity before regurgitating same – Ed.)*

Mais' landscape books make poignant reading today, not just for the sense of peace and quiet that is so hard to find nowadays and for the relative isolation that could then be found just a short distance from the metropolis, but because in many cases one is obliged to arrive by car, the train having long since ceased to serve many of the railheads whence he began his walks. It must say something that reading his guides today makes one want to get up and retrace his steps with all the enthusiasm that he mustered, if only to appreciate what has been lost in the intervening eighty odd years since he produced his first guides for the Southern Railway.

Conducted rambles, such as those led by 'SPB', continued to be offered by the Southern Region well into the 1970s although in the twenty-first century such activities sadly no longer form part of the railway business strategy. A typical offering on 9 January 1972 was a railway journey from London and the suburbs to Farnham, Bentley and Alton. Quoting from the pamphlet, 'Details of organised walks of varying distances are handed to all passengers on the train. On arrival at the country station, parties of moderate size are formed with an experienced leader in charge of each. You may join whichever party you prefer, provided it is not full, or you may plan your own walk. On most dates, moderately priced teas are arranged at convenient points on the organised rambles,' The latter is most surely a facet that would have appealed to 'SPB'!

An editorial note is appended at the back of the book to the effect that, 'While great care has been taken in the preparation of this book, the Southern Railway is unable to accept responsibility for any loss or prejudice arising through any misstatements or inaccuracies contained therein. Further, the mention of any road, footway or bridleway in any part of this text or maps contained in this book must not be construed as indicating the existence of a public right of way. Suggestions for future editions will be welcomed. They should be sent to the Editor, Hills of the South, Advertising Department, General Manager's Office, Southern Railway, Waterloo Station, London SE1.'

A selection of 1970s Southern Region conducted rambles leaflets.

In the Summer of '45

Amyas Crump

Through the efforts of our editor, other contributors and correspondents, we learn regularly about locomotive design and performance, traffic, working, rolling stock, staff working and the history of the Southern in general. We understand that some routes carry intensive commuter traffic, while there were also little used rural lines of considerable charm, but what of those who used the railway?

A recently acquired box of holiday snaps provides the opportunity for a rare insight into the lives of a family of holidaymakers, which may be of general interest or inspiration to those who are modellers. Nothing is known so far of the photographer, G. Lea, or where the family came from, but to have access to a reasonable quality camera and colour film suggests that he was a professional photographer of some sort. Whatever, after the end of six years of the Second World War with all its deprivations, VE Day would have brought forth much relief, and perhaps thoughts of a holiday, and so the couple travelled to Bournemouth, where rooms were booked in a seafront hotel at Southbourne.

Having some traditional July weather, it was soon time for a paddle, although a swim in the sea would have been more difficult with the wartime anti-invasion defences still in place! Although the risk of invasion had long since passed, many beaches still had miles of barbed wire and other anti-invasion measures, such as these constructed from scaffolding to block landing craft, for some time after the end of hostilities. This is Southbourne looking west towards distant Sandbanks and Poole.

Above: Whether it was the motion of the sea crossing, or a shortage of ice cream, even the Mickey Mouse tin bucket has not enthused the younger generation on Ryde beach! I well know these are not railway, but as stated in the introduction the locations are (or nearly all) SR railheads while the rarity of the images plus their historic rarity make them possibly unique. The looks on the faces of those depicted are also poignant, being once again able to relax after the years of turmoil.

Right: Following holidays at Weston-super-Mare and Westgate-on-Sea, a return to the south was made in 1953, with a visit to Yarmouth, Isle of Wight.

Opposite top: Above the beach, along Fishermans Walk, stood a sizeable anti-aircraft gun emplacement, doubtless one of a number protecting that stretch of coastline. There was also time for trips to Poole and Sandbanks. Clearly the holiday went very well and led to return visits in 1947–48. Being more adventurous, these included the local beauty spot at Tuckton, and a paddle steamer outing for a trip to Ryde in 1947.

Opposite bottom: Arrival at Ryde Pierhead coincided with that of the SR's PS *Whippingham* from Portsmouth (and the Red Funnel *Vecta*). *Whippingham* and her sister *Southsea* (lost in the Second World War) came from Fairfields of Glasgow in 1930. At 825 tons and 254ft long they were sizable vessels – a boon on a summer Saturday – being able to carry 1,183 passengers. With their additional bow rudders, they would have been very manoeuvrable, which would have been particularly useful when engaged on their additional excursion duties, which took them to destinations around the Isle of Wight and along the picturesque Dorset coast. *Whippingham* was withdrawn in December 1962 and sold to breakers in Ghent, Belgium, a similar fate to that of so many other seagoing paddlers around that time.

To complete our mini-cruise, we come back to Bournemouth Pier in 1953 aboard a Cosens vessel, the PS *Monarch*, which was part of its fleet from 1951–60 and the second of its ships to bear that name. Built by Thorneycroft at Southampton for the Southern Railway (412 tons, 190ft long), she made the first of many trips from Portsmouth to Ryde in 1924. Surviving in railway service until November 1950, she was a good buy for Cosens at a time when coastal steamer excursion traffic was still buoyant. Eventually competition from the above-mentioned *Swanage Queen* and a general decline in trade led to the decision to sell her off for scrap in 1962.

Opposite: Returning to the mainland, PS *Freshwater* is seen tied up adjacent to the vehicle loading ramp at Lymington in 1956. Built locally at Cowes in 1927, she was much smaller than *Whippingham* at just 264 tons because of the shallow draft needed at Lymington. Lasting until the end of the 1959 summer season, she was withdrawn in the September. There was thought to be still some potential trade for these characterful old vessels and she was sold, to become *Sussex Queen* for the 1960 season. Sufficient profits were not forthcoming and so 1961 found her renamed *Swanage Queen* for a move to Bournemouth in competition with Messrs Cosens, but she was finally scrapped in 1962. In spite of her ultimate loss, she has her place in the founding of the Paddle Steamer Preservation Society.

Terry Cole's Rolling Stock File
No 36 Coach Identification Part 1
Pre-grouping Coaches

In this issue I'm going to look at typical sets of coaches from the three constituents of the Southern and point out differences that, I hope, will be of assistance to the layman in general coach identification. Let me say at the start I shall make some sweeping generalisations and so may offend those who know much more than I do, so please don't inundate the editor with letters. I am approaching the subject from a simple perspective but one that, should the reader wish to know more, will, I hope point him or her to the right place in the many excellent expert books that are now available on Southern Coaches. For the more knowledgeable reader – well, just enjoy the pictures!

Here is a typical LSWR three-coach non-corridor set with M7 No 30052 on one of the typical pre-Hampshire dieselisation workings. A couple more ex-LSWR coaches follow behind. The coaches have elliptical profile rooves with sides that seem to taper inwards towards the bottom, often giving the coaches a slightly top heavy appearance. Typical but not essential features on brake vehicles are sliding luggage doors and curved side lookouts. The non-corridor thirds and composites have toilets dotted along the coach serving pairs of compartments. Many older shorter coaches were rebuilt and lengthened by the Southern and have Southern underframes. The LSWR, unlike the other companies, built quite a lot of corridor stock to the same profile, so if it's 'corridor' it's almost certainly LSWR. Although, of course, the main purpose of the image is the coaching stock, the location can be stated as Swaythling, where the fogman's hut of old sleepers may also be noted. The train is likely to be a down local to Southampton Terminus. *Terry Cole collection*

BR Standard 4 No 76059 heads a typical ex-SECR Birdcage set away from Farnborough North towards Redhill in the mid-1950s. The roof profile is similar to but distinctly different to that seen in the previous view, having more of a 'three arc' line than elliptical. The birdcage lookout on the brake coach is, however, a dead giveaway. The later Birdcage sets didn't have birdcages, just a continuous roof line. The birdcage – basically a guard's look-out, was necessary on the SECR due to its tight loading gauge restrictions, hence it generally shunned side lookouts. The panelling also appears less 'chunky' when compared to the LSWR stock. The composite has a saloon, (a feature the SECR loved), and therefore a different window line incorporating large windows. *Kevin Robertson collection*

H class 0-4-4T No 31518 at Chevening Halt on the Westerham branch in 1960 with a two-coach ex-LBSCR pull-push set. The LBSCR only built simple non-corridor stock until it suddenly produced some enormous 'Balloon' coaches for its mainline express services. Unfortunately, after electrification these were redundant and being too big to be used on the other sections of the SR, were withdrawn. Most of the remaining non-corridor stock was converted to suburban electric sets, which left only the two-coach PP sets on the mainland and a good collection of coaches on the IOW. Note the roof line, which is a simple arc, and also the clean lines of the coach sides. (Many ex-LBSCR coaches were heavily repanelled with steel sheet during their lives.) LBSCR PP sets had internal side corridors and a gangway between the vehicles but this did not alter the window line, which remained typical of a non-corridor coach. Some sets had sliding guards/drivers doors. Toilets were rare. (For more on the Westerham branch, look out for the superb new book coming soon from Crecy and written with much affection by Ron Strutt.) *Terry Cole collection*

The
Southern Way

The regular volume for the Southern devotee
MOST RECENT BACK ISSUES

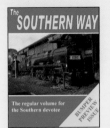

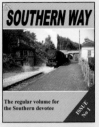

The Southern Way is available from all good book sellers, or in case of difficulty, direct from the publisher. (Post free UK) Each regular issue contains at least 96 pages including colour content.

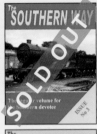

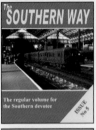

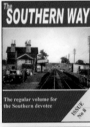

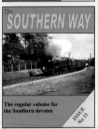

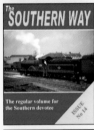

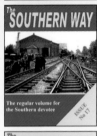

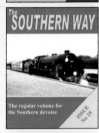

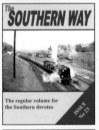

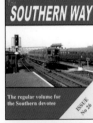

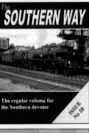

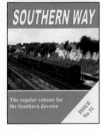

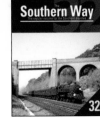

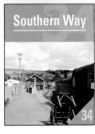
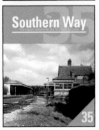
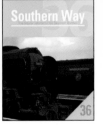

£11.95 each
£12.95 from Issue 7
£14.50 from Issue 21
£14.95 from Issue 35

Subscription for four-issues available
(Post free in the UK)
www.crecy.co.uk